Mothering Heights
(and Depths)

THIS BOOK BELONGS TO BRENDA

Given by the author !!!!

PLEASE ENJOY, BUT DO NOT
REMOVE FROM OFFICE.

THANK YOU!

B.B.

All the best,
Beverly Borgman

MOTHERING HEIGHTS

(and Depths)

by Beverly Borgman

Foreword by Gus Arriola

Illustrated by Peggy Borgman

SUNFLOWER INK
Palo Colorado Canyon
Carmel, CA 93923

(paperback) 9 8 7 6 5 4 3 2 1

Library of Congress Catalog No. 91-061475

ISBN 0-931104-32-7

DEDICATION

To DJ who said:

Why don't you stop talking about it and do it?

And to my wonderful kids:

Patty, Peggy and David

With special thanks to
Ric Masten and Sue Bernhardt

Mothering Heights
(and Depths)

FOREWORD

"Mothering Heights"...The title alone hints of mirth bubbling below the surface, proof that one may well tell a book by its cover. With her witty pick and penetrating lamp, Beverly Borgman has been mining this rich lode since way before "Parenting" became a frayed buzz-word.

Every man knows, 'though few admit, that women have an edge on us, an edge manifest in various ways but none as decided as in coping with offspring. Honing this edge are Beverly's keen observations, documented with a mother's requisite warmth and, above all, Humor.

Not only with her outer and inner eye, she seems to see through our eyes, too, revealing what we may have thought were personal trials with those filial bugaboos, those alliterative "Terrible Twos"or"Turbulent, Tormented, Terrifying Teens".

Hurry! Turn the page and be amused, informed, consoled and, most important, assured....that you are not alone.

Gus Arriola

INTRODUCTION

Or

Wait 'Til YOU Have Kids!

I can see my poor dear mother now, reduced to tears by one of us four children, and striking out with the only weapon at hand:

"Wait 'til YOU have kids!"

Now I know what Mom was talking about. Motherhood is never fully understood until you're smack in the middle of it — rocking a croupy baby, teaching a five-year-old to tie his shoelaces, or standing toe to toe with a teenager who snarls, "YOU'RE RUINING MY LIFE," because you won't let her go out to MacDonald's at 10 p.m.

If you're thinking about becoming a mother, the following chapters may offer a crash course in what it's all about. If you already have kids, you may find comfort in knowing that you're not alone. And, if your children are all grown up and gone, maybe you'd better brace yourself for a return engagement.

Beverly

MOTHERING HEIGHTS*

* And Depths

Honk if you feel guilty

1
Guilt-Edged

When my first child was born, the doctor told me very firmly: "She's big enough to go three or four hours between feedings, so let her cry. Otherwise, you'll spoil her."

Today that doctor would be washing dishes in the hospital cafeteria if he gave that kind of advice. We now know that newborns cannot be spoiled by too much attention or love. Or at least that's the conventional wisdom of the '90s.

I should have listened to my own knotted stomach and aching head some 30 years ago and picked the kid up whenever she seemed unhappy but instead I let an "expert" tell me how to mother. As you can imagine, I'm still carrying a fairly hefty load of guilt for "neglecting" my daughter's cries, but if you think I'm abnormal to still be mulling the question three decades later, well, you just don't know mothers!

Mothers are programmed to feel guilty. In fact, they'd probably feel guilty if they *didn't* feel guilty. Everything they do, you see, is reflected back at them by a child who hasn't the foggiest idea that she (or he) is being observed like a germ in a Petri dish.

Cause and effect is what it's all about:

Did I let her cry too long while I was on the phone? Now she may never trust anyone.

Should we have taken her on that trip instead of leaving her at the sitter's? She may experience a feeling of abandonment in all her relationships.

Should I have given in when she howled for the Crispy Critters at the grocery store? Maybe she'll become anorexic.

On and on it goes:

If I don't buy her the Reeboks she has her heart set on, will she feel unloved?

If I insist that she clean her room at least once a week, will she become a narcissistic perfectionist?

If I forget to tell her that that special boy telephoned while she was out, will she develop a phone phobia?

Guilt, guilt, guilt! How can I be sure I'm not warping her personality in some way if I don't let her go to camp? Will my fondness for candy bars cause her to become obese? If I miss her big win at the swim meet, will she opt to never have children?

If I vote Democratic, will she vote Republican? If I brush my teeth regularly, will she let hers rot?

The fact is, mothers can't win. The very nature of children is to say "No" if Mom says "Yes," to say "up" if Mom says "down," to say "stop" if Mom says "go," but unfortunately, most mothers just never figure it out.

Instead, they continue to assess their "mistakes" and generate guilt like Honda generates cars. I'm convinced that guilty moms could produce enough raw energy to illuminate our major cities but naturally, if they said they liked it light, the kids would say they really prefer it dark.

And Mom would feel guilty about that.

2
The Pain of Having Parents

The kindest thing a pediatrician can do for a young couple is tell them that their adorable baby is not as fragile as he looks, that this seven-pound creature is tough, adaptable and capable of surviving even the most inexperienced parents.

Such survival skills will see the child through teething, croup, mumps and a broken ankle before the age of 12. However, once into the teens, that same kid will develop a strange susceptibility to pain that's directly caused by embarrassment generated by his parents. This is not an embarrassment caused by teasing; this is the embarrassment that parents create just by *being*. The very fact that parents exist is enough to provoke extreme humiliation in the young.

For example, if Mom is 10 pounds overweight, it's embarrassing. If Dad wears polyester pants—even if they're only used for gardening, it's embarrassing. If Mom offers cookies to the kids' friends, it's embarrassing. If she ignores them and goes about her business, it's embarrassing.

If the folks drive a full-size station wagon, life isn't worth living. If Dad barbecues the steaks wearing an apron with a silly saying stamped across it, or if he plays Herb Alpert records, it's to *die*. If the folks stay in the other room when high-school buddies are over, it's embarrassing. If the folks come in and make conversation, life might as well be over.

Even the interior decor at home is subject to teenage disapproval. If the carpet is gold instead of a trendier terra cotta, one might as well have leprosy. If family photographs are hung on the walls, or worse, displayed on the piano, one's whole social life may be at stake.

If there is no hot tub, swimming pool or Sport Court in the back yard, the kids will be forced to just hang around in the street out front and talk about cars. If Mom mentions that she remembers meeting the son's girlfriend when they were both 8 years old and asks, "Didn't she wear braces then?", her son will self-destruct.

If Dad is seen in his undershirt or Mom is seen mending a sock, one's status is endangered. If Mom buys day-old bread and brags about it, or Dad mentions that his favorite sweater came from K-Mart, daughter may stomp out the door proclaiming she'll never *ever* be able to hold her head up in public.

If Dad admits openly that he didn't finish college, or Mom takes a part-time sales job in a department store, it may well be time to run aay from home.

Hopefully, when the kids hit their mid-20s, they'll change their attitude, maybe even come to appreciate the people who are their parents. Eventually they may even forgive the folks for being — *the folks.*

The only parents who will not be forgiven will be those who were too hip, too fashionable, too "with it" — the people who wanted to be "pals" with their kids. Left out in the cold will be the dad who was funnier at telling jokes, who knew more about cars and motocross than his son did, and the mom who was sexier than her daughter — and flaunted it.

What the pediatrician should have told these people many years ago was that a smart parent should always play dumb.

3
Feeling Antsy

When I got up this morning, my husband was long gone to work. On the kitchen counter was a note in his handwriting: "Ants in the bathroom along the shower base. Can you kill them, please?"

I don't know about your house but at mine there are very clear-cut responsibilities. We have no written job descriptions but there is no doubt: I am in charge of ants.

Last month I had to rout them from the freezer, frozen stiff of course, which brought the inevitable question from my son: "Can't they be reconstituted... like orange juice?" Smart aleck kid.

And so I set to work this morning after everyone was gone, placing poison ant-stakes around the perimeter of the house, with special attention to the area near the bathroom. I never once questioned my duties.

It would be different, I thought, if a spider had intruded. Then it would have been "man's work," and if no man was available, I would have left the note: "There's a spider on the bedroom ceiling. Will you kill it for me, please?"

He wouldn't have, though; he'd have removed it gently and deposited it outdoors where it could plan its next foray into the house. My spouse has always had a soft spot in his heart for spiders, ever since he was a teenager and had a pet black widow in a jar, a creature he named Hairy James.

As in many households, when the man of the family travels, such chores as spider eradication revert back to Mom. I recall vividly one evening when a particularly large and ugly spider walked nonchalantly across the family room floor. I was the only adult in the house and the kids immediately climbed up on the back of the sofa, waiting for some solution.

My normal inclination was to run away but thank goodness, the primitive "protective mother" genes came to the fore. I raised my foot as high as I could and came down on the beast with as much force as I could muster.

To my dismay, at least 30 baby spiders hopped off the adult spider and ran in all directions. I looked as if I were doing some kind of weird incantation as I hopped around, trying to eliminate every one of them. The kids, safely perched four feet off the floor, thought it was hysterical. I felt a little hysterical myself.

When it comes to other odd insects and uninvited "guests," I find myself responsible for the removal of sow bugs, earwigs and snails. Mice are another matter. The setting of traps and the removal of same are definitely "guy stuff."

Lizards and snakes, when we have them, must be attended to by children. Adults just couldn't care less — and, more importantly, grownups are not fast enough. Birds, however, are the responsibility of mothers. If the hummingbird feeder is empty, it is she who must cook up a batch of syrup for the little tykes. Mom is also on duty when baby birds fall from nests and must be rescued.

A noisy raccoon in the middle of the night (and any other odd sounds) demands fatherly attention. Meowing kittens at the door, under the house or up a tree are best expedited by daughters.

Last but not least, everyone knows that puppies inevitably attach themselves to small boys, but small boys grow up and leave home, leaving large hairy dogs behind. And large hairy dogs are just like ants — they belong to Mom.

4

Afternoon Delight

It surely must be a sign of old age but when someone whispers "afternoon delight" in my ear, I immediately think of a nap.

Ever since I joined the ranks of parenthood, I know that catching a few winks at midday is the one luxury money can't buy. It's like a throw of the dice: Sometimes you get lucky and sometimes you don't.

As any young mother can tell you, the arrival of a new baby is the time when you most desperately need your rest. Walking the floor at midnight and warming bottles at 2 a.m. take their toll. The next day, after lunch, the body is quivering with the need to fall down and sleep — anywhere!

If the baby is cooperative, Mama may be able to snooze a little but it is usually what I refer to as the Stage One Nap: You sleep with one foot on the floor and the slightest gurgle from the nursery sends you careening down the hall where you suddenly open your eyes and find everything is OK. The baby was just stretching.

Stage Two Naps are the kind enjoyed (?) by mothers of toddlers. In this case, timing is everything. The wise mother sees to it that there is plenty of physical activity in the morning. The little ones are famished by 11 a.m. and finished with lunch by noon. If you can put them in separate rooms (and cribs with very high sides), they eventually sing themselves to sleep and leave you with perhaps two delightful unencumbered hours.

If you're the efficient type, this is when you catch up on all the housework. If you're like me, you just settle for feeling very guilty about not doing those chores and you curl up on the sofa.

If you follow the advice of the women's magazines (Who writes those things anyway?), you'll give yourself a facial, a manicure and soak in a bath of hot perfumed bubbles for 30 minutes — until the doorbell rings and your small one toddles to the front door and invites the Avon lady to join you in the bathroom.

But more than likely, just as you're clearing away the lunch dishes and wiping up the circles drawn in grape jelly, the school "early birds" will arrive home. Bye-bye, nap time.

Stage Three Naps are the ultimate goal of every mother. The kids are pretty big now, and the schools hang onto them each day for as long as they can. This is the opportunity you've been waiting for. Don't blow it. Plan ahead.

A dark cloudy day is ideal. A fire in the fireplace adds a nice touch. Get a big soft blanket, feed the dog, unplug the phone. Put the cat outdoors or he'll walk on your face.

Stretch out on the bed and let yourself go. This is it: the definitive nap. Nirvana.

Suddenly there's a key in the door. Your husband is home early, quite pleased with himself because he knows you'll be overjoyed and surprised that he's come home to start the painting of the kitchen.

It's true; there is no rest for the wicked.

5
Fed Up with Grown-ups

Grown-ups are not rational human beings. Ask any child. Grown-ups are always saying, "No," "When I was your age . . ." and "You've had two already."

Grown-ups are always telling kids that their piece of cake is big enough, that their stack of pancakes is high enough, and that one Big Mac is more than enough.

But grown-ups have this peculiar quirk about food. They keep trying to top each other, and have at various times produced the world's largest banana split, the world's largest "poor boy" sandwich and the world's largest pizza. Grown-ups have actually eaten the world's largest wedding cake, the world's largest hot dog and the world's largest taco. Then they go home and tell the kids, "You've had three pieces of candy already. That's enough!"

Grown-ups are not only into mass consumption; they're also into speedy consumption. There are beer chug-a-lugging contests, pie-eating contests, watermelon-eating contests, oyster-eating contests. And when all that's left is the empty beer cans, the empty pie tins, the empty watermelon rinds and the empty oyster shells, they applaud one another, toast one another, write it up in their grown-up newspapers and put it on their grown-up television.

They even solemnly report when such events go wrong:

"The city of Winnipoo, Wisconsin, was saddened today to lose its champion hotcake eater, Steve Stuffer. Stuffer apparently suffocated when a blueberry lodged in his windpipe. The entire Winnipoo volunteer fire department came to his aid but it was too late."

The grown-ups in Winnipoo will then erect a memorial plaque in the same park where they hold next year's picnic and hotcake-eating contest — but no blueberries next year. Blueberries have been added to the list of possible health hazards. And at breakfast in all the little houses in Winnipoo, grown-ups will tell their children: "Don't gulp your food. Chew it."

Grown-ups are particularly funny about cookies. When their children are hardly more than infants, they tell them, "Walk to Daddy and you can have a cookie." or, "Swim all the way to me and I'll buy you a cookie on the way home."

They give cookies when Baby fusses and they give cookies as rewards for good behavior, and when the child is then totally confused but knows for sure that he likes cookies, the grown-ups change their tune: "Cookies aren't good for you. You eat too many cookies. Cookies will rot your teeth," and they give the kid a box of raisins and expect him to be thrilled.

When the kid asks, "How come *you* don't eat raisins?" the grown-ups tell him not to be sassy.

Grown-ups then go off for vacations, and what do they bring back? You got it. A giant cookie, as big around as a cake, with the youngster's name written across it in frosting.

The child understands that guilt motivated the gift; the grown-ups felt bad at having a good time while the kid was left home with a babysitter who watched soaps all day.

The kid mumbles "Thanks," grabs the cookie and sinks his teeth right into the capital "B" for Bobby. The grown-ups are horrified. "You're not going to eat that huge cookie all at once!" and they make the kid save half for the next day.

Grown-ups are not rational human beings. Ask any kid.

Note Space for Mom

Rx

6
Dog Days

I've been looking at my dog with new respect lately. Until the last year or so, I had regarded him as only a hair machine that was always out when he wanted in, and in when he wanted out.

(I briefly considered a "doggy door" but realized any slim burglar would be able to follow my lovable pet into the house.)

Mr. Spock, as he was named by a 12-year-old "Star Trek" fan, has now been around for nearly eight years, generally underfoot in the kitchen at dinnertime or glaring at anyone who tries to usurp him from the best chair in the family room

He tracks in mud, growls at my friends and until recently I considered his only redeeming attribute his passable skill as a watchdog. Now, to my surprise, I find that having a pet is beneficial to my health.

Medical journals are citing instances of lowered blood pressure and a reduction of stress symptoms when one stoops to stroke a dog or cat. Puppies taken to convalescent homes have wrought remarkable changes in patients who were practically catatonic. Longevity is enhanced, report health newsletters; mental health is restored.

Next we'll hear that fingernails can be stronger if you own a hamster, hair glossier if you raise gerbils, and fallen arches corrected if you adopt a ferret.

Feeling lethargic and depressed? Rub a cat backwards. Lower back pain? Throw out the heating pad and buy a baby pig.

"Look, Mom, no cavities!" and all because the pharmacist came up with an over-the-counter tarantula for Junior. Tamper-proof medication? You bet!

Needless to say, the medical profession is watching all this with alarm. What will happen to Blue Cross, Blue Shield and Kaiser Permanente if diseases can be cured by a visit to an animal shelter?

Doctors are scrambling to cope with the situation. Instead of investing in real estate and limited partnerships, some are trying to corner the market on golden retrievers and Siamese cats.

It's reassuring, however, that the profession is keeping up with the latest scientific developments. At least my doctor is. The last time I complained of a migraine, he advised: "Take two cocker spaniels and call me in the morning."

7

The Lazy Days Of Summer

Maybe you don't care that tomorrow is the first day of summer, that the summer solstice occurs when the sun is at its farthest point north, at the Tropic of Cancer, latitude 23½ degrees north, longitude 18 degrees east, a point which just happens to fall in the Sahara in southern Libya.

That means tomorrow will be the longest day of the year, though perhaps you thought the longest day of the year was the first full day that the kids were out of school.

It has always seemed a little strange to me that in the middle of June, just as we're greeting summer, the days start to get shorter. Maybe it's a symbol for life itself.

Cheap philosphy aside, for many kids the start of summer means more swim meets, more battling over who gets to choose the next movie cassette, and which camp to attend: computer, tennis or "pounds off."

I can remember a simpler summer, a time when houses had shady front porches, and on ours was a faded old couch. I used to curl up on it with books and magazines, and a giant glass of lemonade squeezed from real lemons.

I can remember a bunch of us kids putting on our swimsuits and turning the hose on each other. We'd scream like banshees and run across the squishy lawn until — exhausted — we fell in a heap on the hot sidewalk and let the hose run under us, absorbing the smell of water and cement, and watching the steam rise.

I can remember forming clubs for the express purpose of keeping other kids out, club meetings in sheds or cellars, dark out-of-the-way spots where today's children would never have been allowed to play.

I can remember crowding into my dad's black Willys automobile and being taken to the "plunge" where a nickel bought admission, and another nickel — if you were rich — bought a candy bar with some heft to it, and which, after four hours of swimming, was just about the best thing you ever ate.

I can remember sleeping on the living room floor on hot summer nights when my bed was unbearable. I can remember drinking ice cold chocolate milk, memorable because my mother so rarely bought it.

I can remember getting up at 2 or 3 a.m. to get an early start on a long car trip while it was still cool, and my mother, father, sister, grandparents and I squeezing in for a 200-mile drive over roads that were mostly two lanes.

I can remember a steamy kitchen where my mother, her hair in tendrils on her perspiring forehead, boiled apricot-pineapple jam and ladled it into glistening jars that had rubber gaskets on them. And, once excused from helping her, I remember setting up the big yellow-and-blue beach umbrella in the front yard and selling Kool-Aid at a penny a glass. The mailman, an old German fellow, never bought any but always asked the same question: "Do you have any home brew?"

I can remember helping my mother put the clothes through the wringer on the old washing machine, and being proud that she let me help and scared at the same time that I might get my fingers caught. I also helped her hang the clothes out on the line, handing her clothespins, one by one.

I remember making my own paper-doll clothes by laying the doll on a blank piece of paper and outlining the form, then embellishing and coloring until the most magnificent ball gown emerged, complete with little paper tags to hook over the doll's shoulders.

I remember endless dialogues with our dolls and when that activity paled, we played softball down on the church's vacant lot or hunted trapdoor spiders, or snitched figs from the neighbor's tree.

I'd be lying if I told you that kids in my childhood were never bored, but I don't recall a one that ever developed ulcers.

Note Space for Mom

8
The Omniscient Mother

If the good Lord had intended for kids to get away with murder, She wouldn't have given mothers such acute hearing, keen eyesight and highly developed senses of taste, smell and touch.

Such skills are conferred upon a female the moment she takes her first child home from the hospital. When that tiny newborn first mews its need for food or whimpers in its sleep, it's the mother who hears and leaps from bed as if shot from a cannon.

Maybe it's hormones but from this day forward, it's Mom who exhibits the sixth sense that drives kids crazy — that all-seeing, all-knowing consciousness that continues to function long after the birds have left the nest.

Thus, whether or not they're two years old and into the cookie jar, or 12 and experimenting with beer, Mama is going to *know*.

Granted, on-the-job training hones a mother's senses to a fine degree. She'll notice the strawberry jam around lips that proclaim innocence, zero in on the purple tongue hotly denying knowledge of the missing package of grape Kool-Aid.

Traces of red nail polish that extend all the way to a small elbow may be explained away as scabs but Mom won't be fooled.

As the kids get older, they'll tell more creative stories. If all the apricots disappear from the tree in one day and little Johnny tells of a mysterious stranger in the neighborhood, Mom may just lie in wait for an acute stomach ache to develop.

The mothers who work outside the home develop even keener skills. If small bakers have been at work and attempted to clean up the kitchen before 5 p.m., the almost imperceptible crunch of sugar on the floor will tell the tale.

A car left safely in the garage all day, apparently unused by a grounded teenager, will emit nearly inaudible popping sounds as it cools down. A few blades of grass on the back of a jacket are a good indication that the son or daughter did *not* spend the afternoon at the library as promised.

The CIA would do well to look to these experienced women to swell their ranks. It isn't as if mothers *look* for clues; the clues just seem to come to them.

A working friend, mother of two adolescent daughters, told me recently that she had been putting on her makeup one morning and she grabbed a favorite lipstick and started to apply it. She immediately knew it had been used by someone else. How?

"By its shape," she chuckled. "I figured the culprit had probably dropped it. Then she panicked, cut off the tip and cleaned it."

My friend decided to not confront the perpetrator though she did remark within everyone's hearing that "someone" had used her lipstick.

"No big deal," she admitted to me. "I'll save my anger for something more significant — like an empty gas tank or a door left unlocked.

"Besides," she said, "I don't want to explain how I know about the lipstick. I'd rather have them think I'm omniscient. It's bound to come in handy when they go away to school."

9
It's No Picnic

All hope of ever being The Ideal Mother went out the window years ago when I let the family know exactly how I felt about summer picnics:

Why pack up all that food in a basket, haul it somewhere miles away where the hot things get cold and the cold things get hot? Why battle flies, ants and other crawly things while eating one's meal on a hard bench? Why drag back all the rubbish and leftovers to sort out, and the gooey bowls to wash at home? What's the point — when one could simply put the food on the kitchen table and eat it in a normal comfortable manner?

With my viewpoint firmly established, the kids simply gave up on me and found other families who would take them on picnics.

Naturally, I've felt pretty guilty at times, and looking back, I wonder how I came full circle from those wonderful, lazy summer days when *I* was the kid and the only responsibility I had for a picnic was to be in the car when it left home.

Old photographs show a very young Bev wearng a boy's shirt thrown over some floppy slacks. She's sitting on a picnic table in the deep shade of a sycamore grove. Her head is thrown back in an exaggerated pose and she's about to take a huge bite of a heavily frosted chocolate cake. Calories? She's never heard the word.

The whole family used to go on those picnics — my mom and dad, my mother's parents, my older sister and my two nearly-grown-up brothers and their girlfriends. I usually had a friend along too.

We'd get to the park early to pick out a shady table. Then from the trunk of the car came the goodies — fried chicken, meat loaf, potato salad, Kool-Aid, pickles, olives, maybe a freshly made peach pie and always — the cake.

Impatient beyond belief, my friend and I would escape to the merry-go-round while Mom and Grandma laid out the meal on a checkered tablecloth. If we kids had 25 cents each, we could afford five rides, or maybe four rides and an icy grape-flavored Popsicle that turned our tongues purple.

Then we'd stroll around the park and find a stream to wade in, maybe some tadpoles to catch, but we never wandered farther than the human voice could carry; we might miss the call for food. When it came, we sprinted for the picnic table.

Once stuffed to the point of discomfort, we'd sprawl on the cool grass and listen to the music from the carousel. No blasting portable radios intruded on our soliloquies.

The adults would sit around the table, drinking coffee made in an old blue pot heated over the fire. Picnic conversation was an art, gossip the added spice, but Daddy would inevitably succumb to a nap, his great belly moving rhythmically in sleep as he rested on a blanket safely out of range of any get-up softball games.

Once my friend and I were ambulatory again, we might wander over to the giant walk-on checker-board and push around hub-cap size checkers with sticks designed for that purpose. Or we might amble through the plant conservatory, savoring the lush tropical scents.

It's hard to believe that languid contented picnicker was me, the Scroogish non-picnicking mother of today. The difference between the two? Oh, I'd say about 40 years.

10
The "Blues" Lose

Browsing through a thrift shop the other day I came across a couple of those awful gym suits for girls. You know the kind, the one-piece blue numbers in polyester/cotton with the elastic waist and sagging rear.

Actually, they were better than the other kind, the blue all-polyester stretch jobs with white pin stripes, the ones that made every girl look fat, regardless of her build. I trust those outfits have been banished by now because they made so many young women so very miserable, but I haven't the heart to pick up the phone and call my local high school to ask.

I haven't the heart and I haven't the guts. It wasn't too many years ago that I sat in the principal's office and went toe-to-toe with him over the matter of appropriate apparel for my daughter's P.E. class. It was just after the State Office of Instruction had reluctantly agreed that a youngster need not buy a "uniform" to participate in sports; a shirt and shorts would be deemed suitable.

My daughter, then in high school, was thrilled. She could throw out the above-mentioned outfit and wear something more attractive. She of the long legs and gorgeous tan opted for cut-off jeans.

Apparently, word from the superintendent of instruction was slow in reaching one physical education teacher. She continued to insist on the baggy suits. My daughter's stubborn refusal to conform — based on rights bestowed by the State —was costing her points toward a final grade.

Thus I found myself sitting opposite Mr. Principal and Ms. Gym Teacher, and beside by daughter as we presented our side of the story. "Stonewalling" is the phrase that comes to mind. Both sides were stonewalling: I with a daughter who had the right to wear what she pleased so long as it was safe and decent, and our opponents who steadfastly claimed that the rivets on the pockets of cut-off jeans constituted a "hazard." (No mention was made of the hazard to self-esteem of those who had to wear those awful "blues.")

Actually, I think Mr. Principal was on the fence about the whole thing, but Ms. Gym Teacher had evidently convinced him that his duty was to her in this power struggle between instructor and student.

"Why are you being so obstinate?" he finally asked me in exasperation, unable to see that the same word might apply to his subordinate.

"Because we are within our rights," said I, not at all sure how I had become embroiled in this battle and more than a little surprised that such a small stand of independence by a 15-year-old girl could bring us to such a confrontation.

Ms. Gym Teacher played her highest card; she said that if my daughter did not conform to her rules, she would resign. Quite an ultimatum, a dramatic moment in the evolution of secondary education, to be sure.

I looked at my daughter; she was dug-in for sure. I looked at the thin-lipped P.E. teacher. I looked at the perspiring principal. "I'll leave it up to my daughter," I said. "It's her choice."

I probably don't have to tell you, especially if you've had a 15-year-old daughter of your own, but the next day at P.E. my kid wore her cut-offs, class progressed on schedule, the teacher did not quit her job, the principal went back to worrying about test scores and I went back to work. The crisis was over.

Still, when I saw those gym suits at the thrift shop the other day, I couldn't help wondering if the battle rages on. I also couldn't help remembering how gym teachers since time began have allowed "captains" to choose their teams, player by player, until the poorest, most wretched athletes are left cringing and humiliated on the bench.

Let's hope some things do change.

Note Space for Mom

11
Nature Study

Show me a mother whose kids think she's a monster, and I'll show you a woman who's doing her best to stamp out the pests in her garden.

"Oh, Mom, how can you hurt that little-bitty bug? Look how cute he is when he curls up in a ball." Or, "Look at this adorable baby snail with his little 'feelers' sticking out."

So OK, let's look at this "adorable" snail. I've had to lately; there's been no choice. It's that time of year when the little creatures have my house surrounded and I am being held hostage. In order to get free, all I have to surrender are my petunias, tomato plants, trees, shrubs, oranges, lemons and anything else growing in the immediate vicinity.

They've left no notes but the message is clear, written in the peculiarly silver ink that snails leave behind every morning as they disappear into their shady hideouts.

Considering their destructive capabilities, I'm amazed they have such generally good press. Snail races and snail festivals abound, which leads me to think they have a highly paid public relations person somewhere. What other creature, with perhaps the exception of the jumping frog, has so endeared itself to the public?

Such glorification of a garden pest leads to all kinds of misunderstandings when children catch their parents spreading poison in the garden or worse, stomping the lovable little animals who carry their houses on their backs. But what's so clever about a mini mobile home, and who wants to be buddies with a guy who spreads mucus in front of him to walk on?

I suppose I should be grateful that of the more than 80,000 varieties of snails, our local kind does not grow any larger than it does. Some of the exotic varieties reach a length of six inches! How'd you like to meet that sucker on the garden path?

Snails appear to be amorphous creatures but in truth they have a head, eyes, mouth and tiny teeth. I've no doubt about the teeth, judging by the bite marks on my citrus trees, but it's a little unnerving to think that the snails who paste themselves to my windows have eyes!

Land snails have both male and female sex organs in the same animal. This obviously makes for a lot of confusion and perhaps explains why they favor bedroom windows. Their sea snail cousins, however, are either male or female which probably makes for a group of better-adjusted snails.

According to my encyclopedia, snails are not indigenous to the United States. It seems the French brought them to this country to raise for food and the slippery little critters got away from them. You bet your agapanthus! I think they all ended up at my house.

In an effort to defeat the snails in an ecological manner, I once brought home a duck whose job description was to eat any snails she saw. Unfortunatly, she would not go out hunting by herself; I had to bring the snails to her.

Snails live from two to twenty years. You may have seen some of the older ones. They're quite gray on top, even as you and I, but before you build up any sympathy for one of these poor old fellows, remember, the only good snail is a *flat* snail.

Note Space for Mom

Block parents

12
Block Parents

Did you every have one of those weeks? You wake up at 3 a.m. to the unmistakable sound of croup coming from the nursery, your in-laws have given your son a drum set, and your 13-year-old daughter says she's decided to join a religious sect and hand out flowers at the airport.

You know what you need, Bunky? A Block Parent, that's what.

You've seen the cards in the windows of local homes: Big clear letters spell out "Block Parent." The idea is that a child who, for one reason or another, is in sudden trouble can run to that door, ring the bell and be welcomed by an adult who will offer help. It's a wonderful system, providing immediate assistance against bullies, unleashed dogs and funny old men proffering candy.

My only complaint is that it's limited to children. I know a number of grown-ups, myself included, who would be delighted to have such an asylum.

We all have days when we learn that our roof is going to need replacing, our "baby" has failed kindergarten, or our husband has just hired a 23-year-old blonde secretary who was recently crowned Miss San Diego.

Many of us have been handed the news that we will need varicose surgery, tri-focal lenses, or a salt-free 1,000-calorie-per-day diet. At just such moments in life we desperately need a Block Parent, and here's how it would work:

A kindly woman (maybe even a kindly man if you got lucky) would invite you in, pat you on the head and offer a cup of cocoa — with marshmallows.

"Now tell me, what's the trouble," the BP would inquire. "Is there anything I can do to help? Just sit here by the fire and tell me all about it."

You'd pour out your story and soon your sobs would subside. You might even inquire if there were any cookies to go with the cocoa. Most certainly you'd feel better able to cope with your problems by the time you left.

Perhaps the best thing about a BP for adults would be having someone's undivided attention. It wouldn't be like trying to tell your husband about the stopped-up shower drain when he is watching Monday Night Football. It wouldn't be like phoning your sister when she's in the middle of a home permanent and unable to hear about your impending hysterectomy. And it wouldn't be like calling your mother because, heaven knows, Mother needs a BP all her own.

It may be that Block Parents for Adults is an idea whose time has not yet come, but perhaps all it needs is good financing, a spot on the ballot and a celebrity spokesperson . . .

Maybe Paul Newman.

13
Tee-Pee, Tee-Hee

It's been cold lately and when I woke up the other day, raised the window shade and saw my neighbors' yard totally white, I wasn't too surprised.

Then I put on my glasses and took a second look. Their lawn, shrubs, trees and the roof of their two-story home were not cloaked in ice or snow; they were covered with toilet paper.

In case you're not privy to the social customs of suburban adolescents, a "tee-pee job" on a family residence means that a popular teenager lives there. For parents, it's sort of like having a poltergeist around the place, a supernatural pubescent prankster who drives the family crazy but really means no harm.

I wasn't present the other morning to catch the expressions on my neighbors' faces when they saw their front yard but I'd guess the emotions ranged from a desperate urge to strangle someone to a resigned sigh of relief that no real damage was done.

Of course, the first major storm of the season arrived that same day and literally pasted the tissue firmly to every twig and branch. It's a safe bet that inside that peaceful ranch-style home, the Charmin hit the fan. Because, in case I haven't painted the picture adequately, there was enough toilet tissue used in this exercise to make even Ronald Reagan worry about the finite nature of our forests.

When *I* was a teen, this form of adoration had not yet been invented. We had to settle for a doorbell's ring and flowers left on the front porch, a love note thrust into one's hand between classes, or a simple but impressive majority vote when running for class office.

As with most recently devised social customs, such as coed dorms and women picking up the check, I'm sure the cultural scientists are taking notes and measurements and will advise us soon of the significance of the act. My own research reveals that the inventor of the "tee-pee job" has never stepped forward to claim credit for his creativity.

That's probably a smart move on his part. If the afflicted parents ever got hold of him, they'd wrap him in so much Nice 'n' Soft he'd look like King Tut. Hmmmmm, you don't suppose that's why the teenage Tutankhamen left this world at such an early age, dressed in such an unusual manner...

14
Timing is Everything

The other day I was in the kitchen, working contentedly, a veritable Betty Crocker of the suburbs, when suddenly my doorbell and phone rang simultaneously. A millisecond later, the oven timer went off announcing that the cookies were done.

Alone in the house, I ran to the door to ask whoever was there to please wait a moment while I saved the cookies and answered the phone. It was at that exact point that the tea kettle came to a boil and sounded its frenzied whistle.

Some people would have had a nervous breakdown—but a columnist simply takes notes.

"Timing is everything," a wise man once said. Or could it have been a woman about to embark on the preparation of a turkey dinner? Certainly, timing in my household is crucial with people going to work, going to school and making business trips.

Like any conscientious wife and mother, I find myself the timekeeper and arbiter when schedules conflict. One day last week I lay in bed and slowly opened an eye to look at the clock; it was 6:30.

I heard heavy breathing and knew it was my husband, just back from his morning run and I realized he was later than usual. In another bedroom the clock radio was just starting to waft soothing rock music into my son's ear and I knew that in 60 seconds both of them would be heading for the shower.

I leaped out of bed, cut my son off at his door and threw myself across the threshold. "Don't go in the bathroom," I begged.

He looked at me as if I were crazy, deftly stepped over my prostrate form and went in the direction of the kitchen... another crisis avoided.

Waking is one problem; sleep is another. No one in my family wants to nod off at the same time as the others. Daughter wants to get to bed at 10 p.m. on weeknights, Dad shortly after. Son is addicted to late night TV and doesn't hit the sack until the small hours. Occasionally, on his way to bed he runs into his father who is getting up at dawn because he has a heavy day ahead.

I maintain the delicate balance, reminding those who are awake to be quiet for the sake of those who are asleep and due, no doubt, to the strain, I frequently crash on the sofa in the middle of the day while everyone walks around wondering, "What's *her* problem?"

Meals are just as difficult. Work schedules are erratic, social engagements interfere, and often the dinner I've carefully prepared congeals into an inedible mass before anyone gets home.

Fortunately, I've learned to live with the comings and goings of my tribe but one morning last week the inevitable happened. All four of us turned up at the breakfast table at the same time. It was an awkward moment; no one knew what to say.

You know how difficult it is to eat with strangers.

15

One Big *Happy Family*

I've noticed from reading the business pages lately that there is a definite trend toward making companies into "one big happy family."

It's no longer enough that the employee puts in his or her 40-hour week. Now they must also devote weekend hours every month or so to "business retreats" at out-of-the-way resorts, or attend seminars with a request to bring "the little woman" (or "the little man").

I've run across large groups in hotel lobbies wearing T-shirts emblazoned with slogans like "Ajax Forever" on the front and "Go Team Go" on the back. In meeting rooms where coffee and crullers are served, I've seen perspiring men in regimental ties leading cheers with a fervor usually associated with TV evangelists. The rationale for all this action is to take a disparate group of employees interested mostly in the length of their coffee breaks and the size of their paychecks, and turn them into a finely-tuned machine, capable of expanding production and increasing profits for the stockholders.

Well, I like the idea fine, and if making a company into one big happy family is a desirable objective, why not turn a family into one big happy company? Why not apply the principles of management to the home? Eager for improvement, I turned to an article entitled "Successful Meetings — Management's

Ongoing Challenge."

Oh, how true! How many times, I thought to myself, have I tried to have a reasonable discussion at the dinner table only to have the occasion end in shambles? Here was the key paragraph: "Goals," and listed were "Information flow, decision making, introducing change, upward communication and team spirit."

Exactly. I would let information flow like a river, make decisions regarding house rules, change a few things that were bugging me, let the underlings tell me what they thought. I'd get a team spirit going if it killed me. Even if it meant T-shirts that said "Borgman Rules!"

Before calling the meeting to order, there were things to do. "Prepare an agenda," advised the article. I scribbled down

Dishwasher
Tub Ring
Dirty Clothes on Floor
Telephone

I figured that would be enough for the first meeting.

"Set a maximum time limit," the article continued, "but don't be too rigid. Schedule meetings prior to lunch or at the end of the work day." Saturday morning seemed right to me.

"Select participants carefully." Well, not much choice there but it might be a good idea to call in an unbiased witness who isn't squeamish at the sight of blood.

"Choose the proper setting," the author continued. "Don't schedule the meeting in a place that is too comfortable." Right. The straight-backed kitchen chairs would be better than the living room sofa where my son might doze off and one of the girls might pick up a magazine to browse through.

The article also said to pay particular attention to seating arrangements. "Sitting at the head of the table reinforces a manager's position of dominance but a circular layout can lead to greater contribution by all participants."

Forget the round table, I decided; if I want contributions,

I can go door-to-door.

"To assure maximum attention," said the piece, "hold the meeting where distractions can be kept to a minimum. Translation: "First, put the dog out."

More advice: "Disagreement should not be cut off. However, there is a vast difference between debate and uncontrolled argument." This was not news. That's how the sliding glass door came off its track the last time I tried to discuss how the midnight curfew was being ignored.

Well, Saturday morning came. So did Saturday afternoon. By the time my three teenagers were awake, showered, coherent and available, it was time to start fixing dinner. I decided to scrap the meeting idea and just go back to leaving nasty notes reminding them of chores left undone.

Only now I'll add: "Go Team Go."

Note Space for Mom

16
Mother Talk

"Let's just have a little cooperation here," I said in my most authoritative voice. I was talking to the balky copy machine but one of my young co-workers looked up.

"That tone of voice sure sounds familiar," she said.

I took my cue. "All right, young lady," I responded in a slightly higher pitch. "I think we've had just about enough of that."

She winced.

On a roll now, I added, "If you'd just do it right the first time, you wouldn't have to do it all over again."

"You've really got that routine down pat," my friend grinned. "You sound like a mother."

Well, why not? I've been perfecting it for years—the posture, the tone, the inflection, and once warmed up, I couldn't be stopped. When the sports editor walked by and tossed off a one-liner, I said, "Don't you sass me, young man."

On the way back to my desk I stopped by the religion editor's desk. Surveying her stack of mail and messages, I said, "You'd better get this mess cleaned up. I can't keep this place looking nice all by myself. After all," I added, "you're a lot younger than I am and it's easier for you to pick up those papers than it is for me."

She raised her eyes heavenward in an imploring manner but

she was too busy writing her column to deal with me now.

I moved over to the food editor and volunteered to help proof-read the recipes for Wednesday's food section.

"Maggie! Do sit up straight. If you don't do something about your posture, you're going to have back problems later on."

She yanked the galley proofs out of my hands and said, "Thanks, I can read them myself."

Undaunted, I turned my attention to the book editor who had just gotten off the phone after beating back a publisher's representative intent on gaining an author interview.

"Carol," I said primly, "if you don't take that scowl off your face, you're going to freeze that way."

Her reply was unprintable. Odd, I thought, for a book editor.

I made my way out to the receptionist who doubles as switchboard operator. "Linda, are you *still* on the phone? What if your father had an emergency, tried to call in and the line was busy?"

She pushed her ear piece deeper into her head.

The fashion editor was still in, hard at work on Thursday's layout. I folded my arms and looked her up and down thoroughly. "Lynn," I said in my most serious tone, "don't tell me you're actually going to walk out of here wearing that dress. When I was your age, women were *arrested* for outfits like that . . . Don't you think you ought to button it a little higher and let the hem down a bit?

I left her openmouthed with surprise and scooted off to the cafeteria before she could reply. There I turned my attention to the young woman at the counter.

"Kathy," I scolded, "let me see those hands! Did you wash up before you made that sandwich?" She stepped into the freezer and disappeared.

The managing editor would hear about this. I stormed into his office, interrupting his talk with a reporter. He looked annoyed.

"Well, I shouldn't *have* to knock, Mike. You don't have anything in here to hide, do you?"

He came around from behind his desk, took me firmly by the arm and escorted me out.

"Just wait 'till *you* have kids!" I yelled through his now-closed door.

But I knew he wasn't listening. Kids never do.

Note Space for Mom

17
Castaway

I guess you had to be there. My 13-year-old son was sitting in a bathtub filled with warm water, wearing swim trunks, a smile and a plaster cast on his ankle.

I was on my knees at the side of the tub, intent with saw, hammers and scissors, trying to get the cast off before his dad came home. We made quite a tableau: mother, son and a tub full of wet plaster.

Call it woman's intuition, basic intelligence or a lack of respect for the medical profession; I just knew that the cast was unnecessary and that the doctor had slapped it on hastily for one of three reasons:

1. It wouldn't *hurt* the ankle which had been slightly injured in a basketball game.
2. It would placate me, or
3. It would thrill the kid.

However, as any experienced parent will tell you, the thrill of a cast lasts about 45 minutes. Then it becomes just a cumbersome, itchy bother.

Three days after our visit to the emergency room, I was certain the ankle was OK but the doctor had said the cast must stay on for a week. I decided to get it off one way or another, and I knew I'd have to do it alone. No one else in the family *except* my son would be party to such a rebellious act.

Fortunately, my hunch proved correct and when I finally chopped him out of his cement sock, he jumped out of the tub and ran off to play without a trace of weakness or limp.

Well, why not? He and I had been through difficult times before; the day he was born was one of them. In a simple case of confusion, my doctor had planned his vacation for the week that I was due to deliver. But, he assured me, if by chance the baby did come on time, he had a perfectly good substitute to help me through labor.

"He was on the swim team with me in college; you'll like him." With a reference like that, how could I miss?

Naturally, the baby arrived on schedule, my doctor was 1,000 miles away and the "sub" was called in for the big event. I half expected him to come running into the delivery room in his swim suit.

"Hi," I managed to say as the nurse slipped a mask over my face and I wondered for a moment if it were a snorkel. Fortunately, the delivery went . . . swimmingly.

Six weeks later we had moved to a new community and I took my infant son to a pediatrician who was new to me. Since I'd not yet found a sitter, I also had my two- and three-year-old daughters with me. A starchy nurse took my forms, ushered the four of us into an 8-by-10 foot examining room and told me to undress the baby.

"The doctor will be right in," she told me.

Thirty minutes later the doctor still had not made an appearance and I was holding a wet, naked, screaming baby; my two toddlers were throwing shoes at each other and bouncing off the walls.

That did it. I dressed the baby and stalked out through the waiting room like an angry mother-duck trailing ducklings. No one looked up. I drove home, put the kids down for their naps and earnestly began a post-partum depression.

The pediatrician's office didn't even call to find out what

had happened to me. I'd simply been "misplaced" and needless to say, I lost no time in finding another doctor. Since then, what with moves and all, I've learned a lot about how doctors operate, and I've figured out when to listen and when not to.

So *now* do you understand why I was in the bathroom, on my knees with a saw in my hand, up to my elbows in wet plaster?

Probably not.

CLEAN
FREAK

18
Let's Talk Dirty

I saw a letter in Ann Landers from a woman concerned about her younger sister's squeaky-clean habits. It seems that "Myrna" is in the habit of taking three showers a day, and trying on clothes briefly, then tossing them in the laundry hamper because they are "soiled." She also wears a fresh nightie to bed every night.

Myrna gives further evidence of having gone off the deep end by admitting that if she gets up to go to the bathroom during the night, she puts on a fresh nightie before she goes back to bed.

I'm a lot like Myrna; I can relate to her compulsion to have things clean, to keep everything in order. Otherwise, why would I — *without fail* — clear off the kitchen table every few days just to see if there's anything important under the newspapers and accumulated junk mail?

Like a woman possessed, I sweep away breadcrumbs, orange peels and plates of half-eaten food. I'm the same way with the kitchen sink and counter. I can't *stand* to leave the pork-chop bones, chicken skin and brown lettuce leaves lying around for more than 48 hours. Sometimes I even get up in the middle of the night (shades of Myrna!) to take out the garbage bag which has begun to smell bad and leak from under the sink. Talk about your compulsive types!

Having a pet also complicates the housekeeping problem.

A molting dog demands constant attention. When my dark brown rug begins to go mutt-gray, I send my self-propelled vacuum cleaner on its rounds. Then, of course, there's the necessity of changing vacuum bags, something I do as soon as I notice the bag is splitting. I'm a woman possessed.

I am particularly *driven* when it comes to keeping the bathroom clean. The minute I notice that the ring around the tub is beginning to look like trendy black-and-white decor, I grab the can of cleanser only to find it has solidified from age. (They just don't make those products like they used to.)

I don't like to be catty but I've noticed that some people neglect cleaning their shower stalls. I think it's deplorable, particularly when it's so simple to take one of those little disposable razors and *shave* the mold off the tile.

Even Heloise would marvel at my next idea. Why pay extra for frosted windows to gain privacy in the bath? Simple soap film will make the glass of your windows *and* your shower door opaque in no time.

Like the inspirational Myrna, I'm also very fussy about my clothing. If I wear something once, I hang it inside-out on the clothes hanger so I'll know it's not fresh. If I happen to wear it again, I hang it right-side-out. That way, it may not be fresh, but I'll *think* it is.

I suppose my hang-up with tidiness goes way back to the time when I was a little girl and participated in a PTA program in which I was a "building block" in raising "the whole child." My opening line was, "Cleanliness is next to Godliness."

Who knows what the rest of the speech was, but like some restless ghost condemned to haunt the place of her demise, I now roam the recesses of my home, forever sweeping dirt under the rugs and dust into the corners.

P.S.

While writing this, I suddenly remembered the little sign my mother laboriously printed and hung over the family bathtub. It read:

Oh say can you see
That ring 'round the tub?
Just take that can of cleanser
And give it a rub.
It will not only be
Much better to see
But very much more
San-i-tar-y.

Poor Mom. She never gave up.

Note Space for Mom

19
Sitting Pretty

If I had to add up the good things that have happened in my life in recent years, right at the top of the list would be the fact that I haven't had to hire a babysitter in at least a decade.

With the way the world is going, I'm surprised that anyone still hires a stranger to come in and care for the kiddies, but when I was a young mother, safety from ax murderers and perverts was not my main concern. Getting out of the house was my main concern, and if a snaggle-toothed woman wearing a pointed black hat and clutching a mysteriously bubbling cup of odd-looking cocoa had volunteered to take care of the kids, I would have handed her the baby and run out the door.

That was due to the fact that our small nuclear family always lived at least 100 miles from Grandma's house. Because of transfers and career changes, I never had the opportunity to run next door, drop a crying kid in my mother's lap and say, "I'll be back in an hour." No, every time I needed a break from the graham-cracker crowd, it meant interviewing gum-chewing teenagers who wanted to bring along a friend because they got "lonesome," or hard-core professionals who smoked a pack a night and demanded a four-hour minimum — in cash.

Interviewing sitter candidates was an activity I ranked right up there with cleaning toilets and emptying mousetraps.

As a somewhat shy person, I was always easily cowed by anyone who showed the least bit of aggressiveness. I often found myself apologizing for having only one TV set, only three flavors of ice cream, and for staying out past 10 p.m.

Still, I desperately needed respite from my everyday mothering, and potential sitters were quick to find my weaknesses. Some demanded that the children be fed, bathed and in bed before they would set foot in the house. They were also quick with excuses for problems that developed: "Well, how did I know that your 4-year-old would be attracted to the spray can of silver paint in the garage just when I chose to take a nap?"

Some sitters came prepared to stay indefinitely. It took them an hour to unload the car as they brought in a comforter to sleep under, a thermos of French Roast coffee, a bag full of knitting, six magazines and — most ominous — a small book of telephone numbers of relatives living on the East Coast.

I recall one woman who fed the kids pancakes for dinner, let them talk her into putting syrup, honey and brown sugar on them, then explained that they "must be coming down with something" when we got home and found them sick to their stomachs.

There was also the vague, kindly woman who, after she said good night and accepted her pay, was seen passing our house again and again in the same direction, apparently unaware that she was driving in a circle. I sympathized with her disorientation; the kids had driven me in circles often enough.

Some sitters even snarled at me and demanded that I call before coming home but I rationalized that an evening out was worth some adjustments. I had to admit that as a babysitter myself some years before, I had not been outstanding. I retired from the profession soon after the incident with five-year-old Rochelle; she locked herself in the bathroom with a bottle of fire-engine-red nail polish and wouldn't let me in. I was only 13 myself, and by the time I had called my own mother to help me and Mom had crawled in the bathroom window, Rochelle was vermillion head to toe.

Just remembering that awful day gives me hives but I thought about it recently when a friend told me about a sitter he had as a little boy. My friend and his three brothers were tucked into bed by this woman and told to stay put. The parents were not due home until 2 a.m. The sitter then opened the mother's closet, put on an evening gown and went out on the town.

The parents came home two hours early, long before the enterprising sitter returned, and they were waiting up when she came in. Needless to say, she didn't get paid nor did she get a reference.

Given my assertiveness with sitters, I probably would have apologized for not sending her home in a taxi.

Note Space for Mom

20
Dressing for Respect

One day when I was five or six years old, my mother told me to do something I didn't want to do. I don't even remember now what it was, but I turned to her and said, "Shut up!"

Now, at a much later date and with four well-worn volumes of Dr. Spock behind me, I realize I must have been testing her to see just how far I could go. I found out in a hurry. I also found out that she could outrun me because when I saw the look in her eye, I took off out the back door with Mom in hot pursuit. I ran as hard as I could but she caught me in the front yard and gave me a good whack on the behind.

Looking back, the entire scene was probably pretty funny, a little girl running for her life with a middle-aged lady in a dress and heels close behind. My mother was 43 at the time and no, she wasn't dressed for a job in an office. She was wearing her everyday clothes. That's how mothers dressed in the 1940s, even if it were wash day, ironing day, mending day or shopping day. An apron usually completed the costume.

Today when I put on a dress, stockings and high heels, people ask me if I'm going somewhere special. Usually, I am.

Mom's dresses were not fancy, of course. They were mostly starched and ironed cotton with short or puffed sleeves, and the fabric was a tiny print. As a matter of fact, they looked a lot like what now sells as "organic" clothing at premium prices.

Such attire naturally led to a feeling of respect from the children in the family — with the exception of that one unfortunate "shut up." Who could doubt the authority of a woman who looked so officially adult?

Today it's hard to tell the mother from the kids; they're all dressed in T-shirts, jeans and running shoes. I'm as bad as the rest, but around the house I at least try to see that my T-shirt is pressed, my jeans are clean and my shoes are not run down at the heel.

However, like a lot of people — men in particular — I have a few articles of clothing with which I am reluctant to part: a 10-year-old pair of faded cords, a white T-shirt with my astrology sign and paint spatters across the front of it, and an ageless white poplin windbreaker.

I keep the cords because I've never had a pair of pants that fit so well, the T-shirt because I don't know when I might have to paint something and I don't want to splash paint on something new. As for the coat, I will probably die before it does since it's made of an indestructible polyester, and it's perfect for walking the dog.

Thus there are times when I don't look my best around the house but for the most part I command a certain amount of esteem from my household. Despite occasional setbacks, I do think I am succeeding in my expectations of courtesy and respect from my children. For example, just the other day my son was leaving the house with his date and rather than just walk out the door without saying a proper goodbye, he turned, waved, and said, "See you later, clown."

21
Mother's Little Helper

Around the corner and up the block there's a 15½-year-old boy who has just gotten his learner's permit to drive. I can tell because I see the family sedan lurching out of the driveway with him at the wheel and his mother clutching the passenger door with both hands.

As the boy stalls the engine just in front of my house, his mom attempts a casual wave of greeting in my direction, but even at 25 yards I can see the whiteness of her knuckles. As they turn *left* at the bottom of the hill I notice that their *right* signal indicator is blinking.

No one has to tell me: Junior is "helping" his mother by taking her to the grocery store, the store to which she has driven three times a week for the past 20 years, the store which she could find in a blizzard with her eyes sealed shut.

Later on today Junior will probably volunteer to take his little sister to the library, the same sister he punched in the mouth just before he went to the DMV to get the learner's permit. And this evening he'll no doubt offer to deliver something to Grandma's house, the same Grandma he has seriously ignored since he turned 12.

This model son, this perfect example of juvenile decorum will of course have to ask an adult driver to accompany him but he'll be so persistently pleasant that it will be impossible to refuse him.

Six months down the line it will be another matter:

Driver's license firmly in hand, he'll disappear with the family car for hours at a time. A five-minute errand to the drugstore will use up the afternoon, a trip to the recycling center will consume an entire Saturday and a tank full of gas.

Attitude? "Surly" best describes it — and the mirrored sunglasses don't help. He'll stand in the kitchen with his hands pushed deep into the pockets of his black leather jacket, his mouth a thin line of contempt, while Mom tries patiently to work out a schedule for the car that *everyone* can live with.

Once in the car (now decorated with every rock radio bumper sticker known to man) and no longer in view of his house, he'll put the pedal to the metal. The car windows will be down and the car radio up. Tires will screech and small children on the sidewalk will jump back instinctively. The Dr. Jekyll and Mr. Hyde of the neighborhood, the fellow for whom all insurance companies lie in wait, will leave a path of burnt rubber behind him.

The State of California, in its infinite wisdom, has declared that all youngsters of 16 are capable and responsible enough to drive automobiles. I've only heard of one parent who ever stood her ground, declared her child unsafe on the streets at that age, and refused to sign for him. I don't know what happened to her and I shouldn't like to ask.

However, the 15½-year-old kid driving his mother down my street today is the same one I saw last summer, riding his skateboard backwards down a hill toward a blind intersection. He's the one whose jeans are so tight he'd never be able to bend his knee enough to brake in an emergency.

I wave a cheery hello to his mother as he gets the car started again, and give her a thumbs-up sign. Mom, this too shall pass.

22
Winter Sports

I guess I'm not the outdoor type. One recent night at dinner I mentioned that I might like to try cross-country skiing. My husband and son went into such paroxysms of laughter that they couldn't eat their dessert. I was so upset that *I* could hardly eat their dessert.

Somehow people don't envision me on ice skates or skis but I've been involved with other winter sports for a long time.

Surely you've heard of the "Muddy Dog Race." It's an event played mostly by mothers and involves a starter (your child) who opens the door and calls in his pet. Mother then runs from the most distant point in the house and hurls her body between the dog and the newly waxed kitchen floor. Points are awarded for speed.

Small children can participate in the "Mitten Search." Any number may play and points are awarded for the mitten found in the sleeve of the jacket lying under the bed.

The "Hat Hassle" is another indoor winter game played by parents and children ages 2 to 12. This is an endurance contest. "Put on your hat if you're going out." "I don't want to." These phrases are repeated over and over again and the last person to speak is the winner.

The "Soccer Drive" is another test of endurance in which mothers drive endlessly from field to field searching for the game in which their child is supposed to be playing. Points are awarded for giving six other kids a ride home. Bonus points go to mothers who can never drive on rainy days.

Some people prefer water sports, even in the winter. The "Hot Tub Crawl" is a stroke popular with suburban mixed doubles.

I am particularly good at the "Firewood Lift." This event builds biceps and is generally played alone until the wood is in the fireplace. Striking the first match signals other participants to join in.

The "Budget Downhill Event" generally follows the "Mall Marathon." The marathon takes place in early December and is usually played by children doing Christmas shopping. Older players who walk up and down the mall wearing glazed expressions serve as referees.

January brings the popular "Clearance Sale Sprint" with rules similar to the marathon but the players are adults. Like ice hockey, this sport sometimes gets ugly and fouls are not uncommon. Exhausted athletes often come home after this event and execute the "Cold Shower Scream." The contestant steps into the stall after four other family members have showered and washed an endless amount of hair. A very high decibel count is the mark of a champion in this event.

Winter is also a popular season for the "Vaporizer Hunt." In this game the participant who was "it" during the flu epidemic in May hides the vaporizer and challenges the contender to find it in January.

The popular "Thermostat Hurdles" continues to attract husband and wife challengers, one of whom sets the thermostat at an energy-conserving level, and the other must try to turn it up without being caught. It's good clean fun, with PG&E the winner.

The highlight of the season is the ever-popular "Charity Olympics" in which phone calls from faceless strangers invite you to collect money for worthwhile charities. Generally, they invite you to collect from "just 10 houses in your neighborhood" and it all sounds so reasonable. But last year, after hitting those 10 houses in a frigid rain, I decided I'd give up winter sports and just sit arund the house and watch my skin crack.

Note Space for Mom

23
Kid, Kid, Who's Got The Kid?

It's a sign of the times, I think, that the census taker came to our door a minimum of six times in 1990. When one fellow got totally confused, the government sent another in his place. In this case, it was the rearrangement of street numbers in our area that had them crazy, but I predict that the most confusing aspect of the final count will be the discovery of a whole new category — the kids who have moved in with other families.

Take a look at your own neighborhood; the adults aren't moving but the children are. They change houses so frequently that it's hard to tell where anyone resides anymore or who belongs to whom.

It seems that most young adults can live with just about anyone except their own parents so the obvious solution appears to be to simply trade kids, and the sooner the better. Why keep the little critters around 'til you get attached to them? Move 'em out when they're five or six.

Who knows? The family up the street may think you have absolutely charming children and they'll be happy to trade the losers they were stuck with by the accident of birth.

I think we're on to a significant change in our societal structure but we should have seen it coming. There's not a parent alive who hasn't had to hire a neighbor kid at least once to do the household chores that his own kid evaded. When his offspring went limp at the idea of washing the car or mowing the lawn, it was not only expedient but perhaps a moral victory to hire the kid across the street.

Sure, he could have paid his own son or daughter to do the same chore but these famous words have been uttered more than once: "You're a member of this family; we shouldn't have to pay you to help around the house!"

The Jones kid across the street (we'll call him Chester) was an absolute slug in his own house. He never rolled out of bed on a Saturday until 2 p.m., never picked up his own clothes or put his dirty dishes in the sink. Chester's whole self-image was wrapped up in doing nothing, and doing it with panache.

But the minute the Smith family across the street waved a $5 bill in front of him and asked him to rake leaves, Chester became a workaholic, camping on the Smiths' doorstep at 7 a.m. Saturday mornings, washing their car sometimes just for the fun of it.

Meanwhile, Chester's parents, who were still picking up after him at home, watched in amazement. In self-defense, they hired the Smiths' kid (we'll call him Merrill), who was thrilled to clean roof gutters for them or prune the fruit trees in the back yard. (Chester hadn't even *seen* the back yard since he was 10.)

Eventually, Chester moved his clothes, stereo and weight-lifting bench across the street to the Smiths', and Merrill moved his guitar, amplifier and '57 Chevy over to the Joneses.

The Joneses are happy with the arrangement, and the Smiths don't seem to mind, but I have a hunch Uncle Sam's computer will crash when he tries to sort it all out.

Note Space for Mom

24
An Uncontrollable Urge

I think I'm coming down with something. It's one of those ailments that hits regularly in July or August, like a summer cold. I have this uncontrollable urge to hug little boys! *Very little* boys, about one or two years old.

Sure, the little girls are cute too but the little boys are irresistible — maybe because my last baby, born more years ago than I care to count, was a boy.

I see them everywhere but it's mostly at the swimming pool that the urge overtakes me. They're wearing tiny bright swim suits and they look like little dumplings, still rolling in baby fat.

The ones who are just learning to walk are the best. Like miniature drunks, they ambulate precariously, occasionally slipping on the wet decking but they're built so close to the ground that the tumble is hardly noticed.

Sometimes you'll find one asleep in a play-pen in the shade, his chest moving in and out regularly while a glistening bead of perspiration forms on the softest of chins. Some are bundled up in white terrycloth, only a little face showing, shivering slightly and waiting patiently while mother puts on her sandals to go home.

I find myself sitting nearby where I can watch these small beings and sometimes I'll venture a friendly "Hi" which often sends them screaming to Mama.

On warm evenings you'll find them being towed through the water by their daddies, shrieking with delight at the bubbles they are making together.

They are the most *huggable* things — the babies, not the daddies — and like some rare species, you have to watch for them and enjoy them while they are in season. The next year you may not recognize them at all as they clutch at their mothers' legs, whining for an ice cream bar and behaving in a generally unsociable manner.

Worse yet, three or four years down the line they are jumping into the pool with great glee, as close as they can get to ladies like me, in order to splash and annoy. At the age of 10 or so, they have become thoroughly obnoxious, grouping like guppies to bully the smaller boys and harass the girls.

From 12 to 14 they spend a lot of time "benched" — put out of commission by the lifeguard who says either they respect the rules or they're "OUT!"

At 17 their suits are once again pared down to the size they wore when they were 18 months old. Their hair is styled, they glisten when wet, ripple their muscles and execute difficult dives in order to attract young females. As for women my age, they simply *step over* us when we happen to be in their path; we are nothing more than a lump in a beach towel.

How wonderful though that every year there is a new crop of clumsy, beautiful little baby boys that appear at poolside where they can be thoroughly enjoyed. Otherwise, I might start thinking about having one of my own.

25
Like Mother, Like Daughter

I had lunch with a friend the other day. We must have downed a full pot of coffee as we lingered for at least two hours. When the waitress began tapping her foot and looking at her watch, we figured out our bill and left what we hoped was a generous tip.

My friend and I had covered everything that had happened in the month since we'd last seen each other, but mostly we talked about our kids. Having a friend who will listen to your child-rearing problems sure beats paying a shrink $75 for 50 minutes. Another mother who's in the same boat is about the best safety valve a woman can have.

I'd just told my companion how my 15-year-old daughter had sneaked out of the house to go to a midnight showing of "The Rocky Horror Picture Show," and she said she understood completely. Just when she'd gotten used to her 14-year-old son's shoulder-length hair, he'd had it shaved into a Mohawk.

"How long is it going to be like this?" I asked rhetorically "I'm losing my mind."

My friend was stoic: "It's only adolescence," she said. "In a few years they'll be like real people . . . Don't give up hope."

I went on to tell her about my son bringing home a borrowed drum set and installing it in his bedroom, and she was filling me in on her latest trip to the hospital emergency room when

I noticed two 12-year-old girls at another table.

They were talking about their parents; family secrets were being openly discussed and each girl occasionally giggled wildly. I leaned forward to catch more of the conversation. "Elsbeth" was saying:

"My mother screamed so hard yesterday at my little brother that she lost her voice. Then when her boyfriend complained that his TV dinner hadn't heated all the way through in the microwave, she tried to yell and couldn't even whisper. She got so mad that she threw a plate of french fries at him!"

Elsbeth's little friend "Tiffany" nodded knowingly. "Aren't adults ridiculous? My father turned on the late-night cable movies after he thought my mother was asleep. She caught him watching and ran back to the bedroom and locked the door. Poor Dad had to sleep in the den."

"My dad," sighed Elsbeth, "got his hair permed, and dyed the gray back to brown. He acts like no one will notice — and he's been lifting weights and jogging five miles a day. What's he trying to *prove*?"

"Oh, you know," said Tiffany, rolling her eyes. "They have all those hormones rampaging through their bodies when they're that age. You just have to be patient with them."

"I try," said Elsbeth, "but you wonder sometimes if they're ever going to grow out of it."

26
The Music Lesson

I've always thought that behind every great musician there probably was a mother who made sacrifices, both emotional and material, so that the world might come to know her child, The Artist.

Therefore, it's interesting to note that when I was 10 and showing an interest in music, my mother gave away our piano. She loaned it to the USO "to further the war effort," but when World War II ended, she never bothered to reclaim the instrument. Nor did she replace it.

Now that I have a son in the house who is a budding musician, I understand my mother a lot better. I also understand why mother birds throw their musical darlings out of the nest at a very tender age — their nerves can't hack it.

They say that Johann Sebastian Bach at age 12 was sneaking difficult musical manuscripts into his room at night to copy. Ludwig van Beethoven was giving concerts at age 13, and Frederic Chopin at 17 was recognized as a talented composer and the leading pianist of Warsaw.

I'm not sure if these three boys had mothers or not but I am sure that someone in their households was biting her nails a lot and having recurring headaches.

The guitarist in my house, though not a child prodigy, has the kind of dedication that makes for success. He practices from morning 'til night, grudgingly giving up a few hours to go to high school. He draws countless little black dots in lined notebooks and twice weekly he visits the music store as a neophyte would visit a shrine.

He has struggled beyond the rented $40 acoustic guitar through several levels of electric models. His amplifiers have become increasingly more expensive and sophisticated, capable of extending indefinitely the length of a musical note or distorting it beyond recognition.

His current electronic system sits hunched in my living room like a large monster with one red eye, sending piercing screams to the most distant parts of the house and causing the pictures on the wall to hang crooked.

My resident musician has passed the era of simple John Denver melodies and is more intent on mastering Lydian dominant scales and augmented ninth chords. Don't ask me what that means; I just know that I'm a lot more nervous that I used to be.

My son continues to take lessons, siphoning off whatever he can from whomever will teach him. He also uses current rock albums to teach himself. The albums are as costly as the lessons. With a habit that must be satisfied, he has cleverly figured out how to keep some cash coming in: He teaches others.

Every afternoon there are little "rockers" coming to my door hoping to emulate members of the latest hot group. They arrive with their guitars strapped to their bikes. They sit in the big living-room chair, some so small that their feet don't reach the floor.

They come with high hopes and are inevitably disappointed when the first song they must learn is "This Land Is Your Land," but my son convinces them that even Rod Stewart had to start somewhere.

In the beginning there was only one guitarist in my house. Now there are at least 20. When it comes to encouraging and inspiring, I seem to have outdone myself.

27
General Hospital

If you're looking for cheer today, I suggest you go elsewhere. You're dealing with a woman who's about to snap.

One of the young "boarders" in my house has had bronchitis for three months. The sound of her coughing has reverberated through the furnace vents for weeks and I'm sure that's what has caused the new cracks in the wall. During her illness I've become letter-perfect on the physiology of the pulmonary system; given a blackboard and chalk, I could lecture for hours on the bronchial tree, the lungs and the cilia.

The family medical guide has grown dog-eared from constant use and words like tuberculosis, bronchiectasis and pneumonia have replaced the usual subjects of winter conversation — like budget, PG&E and hot water. The pharmacist, radiologist and lab technician have all become close friends.

While gulping Vitamin C in wholesale quantities and doggedly walking the dog a mile a day, I suddenly noticed that the other young person in the household was looking green about the gills. A little pain in the gums turned out to be an infection complicated by four wisdom teeth growing in four different directions — north, south, east, west but not *out*.

"The infection will have to subside before we can remove the teeth," the oral surgeon said as he handed over a prescription that cost $36.75. How could he do this to a person who remembers when a day in the *hospital* cost $35?

"What do you prescribe for shock?" I asked weakly.

"Plenty of dental insurance," he grinned.

After a week, the angry gums had calmed down and the wisdom teeth were extracted. A once-handsome young man now looked like a six-foot chipmunk as he alternately wandered about the house in his jammies or lazed in front of re-runs of "Star Trek." Unable to open his mouth for solid food or intelligible conversation, he grew increasingly restive as his sister continued her unceasing bronchial bark and began an addiction to Sucrets.

As for me, I escaped to the office whenever I could, where the howl of an editor and the roar of the presses lulled me back to temporary sanity. That is, until today when I woke up with a sore throat and a runny nose. I rolled over, turned off the alarm and turned the electric blanket up to 10.

If you can't fight 'em, you may as well join 'em.

28
The Leisure Class

At my house this last three-day weekend, my teenage son and his girlfriend began work on a jigsaw puzzle. Using a large piece of posterboard as a base, they started to assemble the 500 pieces on the bedroom floor, then moved it to the living room coffee table for a more comfortable spot.

It was a nice, relaxed endeavor for a holiday afternoon, in pleasant safe surroundings. No parent could reasonably object to such an activity. Why then did I feel the hair on the back of my neck rise when they first started carefully laying all the pieces face up?

I think it was jealousy.

Nearly everyone envies the young their vigor, their looks and their energy. I envy them their time. That's not to say they're not busy with school, jobs and car maintenance. It's their approach to time that I covet, the feeling that they have as much of it as they need and if not, they can always find more.

I remember having the same attitude. Life is unrushed for those who refuse to let themselves be pushed, and these kids knew that a holiday is just that — a holiday. They weren't going to waste it sneaking extra loads of clothes into the washer or getting the jump on a history assignment. If the chores piled up, so what?

I used to have that same *laissez-faire* approach to life.

Before I consumed 30 years of women's magazines, I used to just sit sometimes, my hands idle in my lap, or I'd lie on the sofa, a novel resting on my chest. I didn't know I was wasting time 'til I read all those articles on how to get more done every day.

In a zealous effort to shape up and improve my efficiency, I stopped just short of washing the babies with the clothes, but I learned that you can catch up on correspondence while waiting in the dentist's reception room, you can strengthen and tighten your buttocks while typing for the boss, and you can visit by phone with your mother while cooking dinner — if the telephone cord is long enough.

I've become a whirling dervish of accomplishment. True, long relaxing games of checkers or chess have become extinct, but I've come to the point where I think a Scrabble game is still fun, even with a 30-second limit for making words.

In fact, given a jumble of letters, I could probably spell l-e-i-s-u-r-e in that half-minute — but I'd be hard put to explain what it means.

29
Happy Campers

It seems appropriate to confess at this time that everything I write is not always totally accurate. Sometimes the names are changed to protect the guilty. Sometimes the date is changed because the memory is faulty. Sometimes the facts are embellished because, after all, life is not always that interesting.

Having made that disclaimer, let me now tell you that the following is a factual, complete and unadorned report of my week at summer camp:

For the past 10 years my family has been going to camp together. Don't ask me why. It may be laziness, a lack of creativity or simply an easy way to avoid a big argument. At any rate, we pack up and we go.

This year we arrived on Saturday afternoon and on Saturday night I took a fall and injured my ankle. It happened just at the end of the campfire and after the singing of the alma mater.

Breakfast in the dining hall the next morning was interrupted by the announcement that Stan, a middle-aged camper, was driving his nephew to the hospital 20 miles down the mountain. The boy had fallen out of an upper bunk and broken his wrist.

A day later Stan himself was hobbling about and avoiding all strenuous activity. His back had gone out. Whether due to some physical exertion or just plain stress, I never found out — but his nephew who was wearing a cast seemed unimpeded in his pursuit of Fun.

A day later Rob, a young and vigorous camper, fell ill with a 24-hour-bug. The same fate befell a tiny one-year-old camper and I could imagine how much fun his mother was having, doing nursing duty in a dusty tent.

I think it was Wednesday that Tassie, a popular young woman who was the picture of vitality when she arrived four days earlier, was bitten on the eyelid by an insect while on the all-day hike. That evening her eye had swollen shut and she was holding an icepack to it.

That same night Jeff and Susan in Cabin 36 spoke to the camp doctor about their daughter Shelley. The doctor diagnosed either strep throat or mononucleosis and prescribed bed rest.

The person I felt sorriest for was Jane, mother of three teenagers. I noticed her hobbling about on crutches and saw that she had difficulty negotiating the stairs of the dining hall and the restrooms.

When I asked what awful mishap had befallen her, she replied that she had been on crutches when she came to the mountains and she was planning to have surgery later in the year for a hip disorder. Maybe she thought she'd be less conspicuous at camp than she would be on the streets of her hometown.

She was right. By week's end Jane looked like just another happy camper.

Note Space for Mom

Twinkies

30
For the Birds

You are looking at someone who's just had her nest emptied and it's not a pretty sight. My mascara is running and my eyes are red. My last child has left home.

My refrigerator is stocked with things that may never be eaten — frozen Twinkies and orange-flavored punch, and the mess in the bathroom is all my own.

I had visions of diving right into all those chores I'd saved this past summer but I find myself pulling the sheets off his bed and snuffling into them like some demented degenerate.

I started to clean off his desk and found little notes he had written to himself, reminders of things to take. The room itself gives the appearance of having been left in a hurry and I am walking back and forth to the laundry room, picking up dirty clothes that were under the bed.

He left behind a large stack of Guitar Player magazines and entertainment listings of rock concerts. I've sucked up half a dozen guitar picks with a vacuum cleaner; they're exactly the same color as the carpet.

His amplifier and huge four-speaker cabinet went to college with him. So did two guitars and numerous extension cords and sound-distortion gadgets. I also noticed a couple of books packed in his suitcase" "Basic Guitar, Volume I" and "Basic Guitar, Volume II." Somehow, these were not the books I imagined him reading in his dorm room.

Left behind in his closet was the neatly pressed three-piece suit he wore to the high-school homecoming dance. Gone with him are all the blue jeans he ever owned. Gone also are the mostly black T-shirts purchased at concerts and considered by his peers to be very "bad," which of course means very good.

My car, the one that was usually parked at the music store, at his part-time job or at his girlfriend's house, stands deserted at the curb. The quarter tank of gas he left me will probably last the month.

Today I shopped in a leisurely way at the supermarket, choosing items that he never liked. I also bought dinner-for-two specialties. I expect my grocery bill, my water bill, my PG&E bill and my gasoline bill will all drop considerably. When I hear people talk about the exorbitant cost of sending kids to college, I wonder if they ever figured out what it would have cost to keep them at home.

It's not as if I couldn't wait to get rid of him. After all, this is my "baby," the little guy who was born with a perfect Ivy League haircut, who used to lay his head on my shoulder, absolutely content to be cuddled. And as a big guy, he was exceptional in that it never embarrassed him to give me a hug in public or to say "I love you."

Well, shucks, it isn't as if he's gone away for good, I'll no doubt see him in a month or two. It's just that the house seems deserted; certainly, the music is gone. And while I know I'm supposed to be reveling in all this marvelous freedom, all this peace and tranquility, I think I liked it better the other way.

Empty nests are for the birds.

31
Past Imperfect

I ran across an old snapshot recently, a picture of my daughter when she was nearly three years old. There she stood with cotton swabs sticking out of her ears and nostrils. Fluffs of dust hung from the swabs because she had found them under her bed.

It was Peggy's way of diverting my attention from a new baby boy.

The snapshot started me thinking about how idealistic I had been before I had children. My husband and I were going to raise the perfect child — a clean, cheerful little creature whose nose ran, who never whined in the supermarket, and who never ran, who never whined in the supermarket, and who obeyed instantly. We'd never have to raise our voices.

We had seen all those horrible examples of other people's children and we knew it was just a matter of discipline mixed with the right amount of understanding. *Our* child would be different.

Shortly before we had our first baby, we paid a visit to friends who were parents of two develish little boys. The young father had just acquired a beautiful Brittany spaniel, and he was showing off the dog to us, demonstrating that the spaniel would wait beside his food dish and not eat until he was given the command.

Heady with power, the father suddenly had a new thought: "You know," he mused, "if you can train a dog, you should be able to train a child."

Ten years later he was still trying to apply his theory, but his teenage boys were putting him through hell.

The realization of powerlessness came early for me; my first child was a colicky baby from her first day. No amount of attention or *in*attention could soothe her. She simply turned red and screamed for hours.

The siege seemed to me to be a sort of "basic training" for parents, a "boot camp" of the booties set. After surviving that first month with Patty, anything would be an improvement.

Well, it didn't quite work out that way. With three children, we went through emergency trips to the hospital, heavy colds with their attendant runny noses, facial impetigo, allergies, asthma, head lice and other physical unpleasantness with which every parent is familiar.

As far as behavior was concerned, I had my share of phone calls from angry neighbors, teachers and principals, and was even faced with a hostile postal carrier when his truck was robbed of toothpaste samples by my four-year-old "Butch Cassidy" and his three-year-old buddy from next door, the "Sundance Kid."

As for manners, it was always touch and go. I tried to instill the basics such as where the fork goes, don't lick the knife —especially if it's sharp — and don't blow your nose in your napkin.

In an effort to be thoughtful, they agreed to not call me "the old lady" or "toad."

A few weeks ago, after not hearing from my son at college for quite a while, I anxiously answered the phone's ring. The operator asked: "Will you accept a collect call from David?"

"Yes, I will," I responded, happy to hear from him but a little worried too.

"Er, ah, hello," he said. sounding kind of embarrassed. Then he admitted, "Gee, Mom, I was trying to call my friend Jim and have it billed to your phone. I guess the operator got mixed up."

"Well, as long as I have you on the line," I said, ignoring the slight, "how are you? What's new?" And I launched into friendly conversation.

As any parent of a non-perfect kid will tell you, you take whatever you can get.

Note Space for Mom

32
What's Cooking

I knew I was in trouble when I got out of bed yesterday and tripped over the pancake griddle.

Nursing my bruised toe, I observed that the blender was on the night table, Mr. Coffee was high on a closet shelf with my shoes, and my large stainless mixing bowl was on the carpet by the bathroom door. Everything was right where I'd left it.

I had my usual light breakfast. The corn flakes box was under the dining room table, the sugar was on a plant stand, and I fished a spoon out of a cardboard box in the entry hall.

I made a sandwich for lunch using the window sill as a cutting board, and found a package of cookies in my scarf drawer.

What's frightening about all this is that it's beginning to feel normal. That's because I am "The Lady Who Is Having Her Kitchen Remodeled" and I'm mad as the Hatter, as crazed as Lady MacBeth. I'm no longer capable of lucid conversation. If the subject is politics, I may say something entirely irrelevant such as "tile," "wallpaper" or "soffit." If the subject is sports, I'm just as likely to interrupt with "plaster" or "double panes." If the subject is remodeling, I break into nervous giggles and have to be forcibly calmed.

I haven't had a real meal at home for four weeks. I've been washing dishes in the bathroom sink for so long that I only occasionally notice after my bath that I'm toweling off with a piece of red-and-white gingham embroidered with a tea pot. My natural desire to provide the family with the basic four food groups has been reduced to grabbing chili-to-go in styrofoam bowls at the corner pub.

My dog, a wonderful guardian of all I possess, is totally confused as I scold him for threatening strangers who walk right into my house and proceed to knock out a wall. He skulks off to his doghouse with a posture that suggests, "Well, make up your mind!"

I'm up at 6:30 every morning making myself presentable for a contractor who is a friendly fellow and a great kidder. "I'll be there at 8," he tells me cheerfully, but neglects to add that he means Tuesday, not Monday. "We'll work a full day tomorrow," he says, but omits the fact that he means from noon to 9 p.m.

A brand new electric range is installed, the oven light won't go off, and I'm told I must wait five days for a service call. I buy wallpaper and find I need more, and the pattern has been discontinued.

I now understand the expressions I saw on people's faces before this whole project began. When I told them happily that it was going to take a week — two weeks at the most — to complete the job, they smiled knowingly and said, "That's wonderful," using the same tone that one uses to coax a jumper off the bridge. Not one person, not even my nearest and dearest friends, tried to talk me out of my plans. It was as if the Cone of Silence had dropped over them.

Today if someone asked me if she should have a baby, I'd say, "Well, maybe," and if someone asked if she ought to have cosmetic surgery, I'd say, "Perhaps," but if anyone asked me if she should remodel her kitchen, my answer would be swift and unequivocal.

It just wouldn't be printable.

33
Baby Boom A Bust?

Is it my imagination or are there a lot of babies being born these days? At the grocery store I can't help but peek into the soft blankets to see those tiny hands. At the shopping center I nearly dislocate my spine peering into these new high-tech strollers to see the wizened little faces of creatures who have just joined the human race.

Once I've satisfied my curiosity about the child, my gaze shifts to the mother, and more and more often I am seeing a mature woman who is nearly 40, a woman who obviously has *chosen* to be a mother, a woman who looks as if she knows exactly what she's doing.

Often she's a person who has attended classes to help her decide the question of whether or not to become pregnant. She has examined the pros and cons, had ultra-sound to determine the health and the sex of the baby, and perhaps even amniocentesis, that rather awesome procedure that further assures that postponing the maternal experience has not endangered the child. In other words, all systems are "Go" for raising a youngster who is wanted, planned and included in the budget.

This Mom of the 1990s leaves little to chance. More than likely she is a careerist who has kept her maiden name and who hopes to get back on the fast track in six months or so. Her life-plan resembles a flow chart, her little one the wonderful manufactured "product," and the proposed "bottom line" a series of satisfying vignettes in which she plays the role of proud parent.

Compared to the unsophisticated, pregnant 18-year-old, Ms. Professional appears to have the world by the tail. No rough spots for this goal-oriented executive; having a child is just one of the things she planned to do, and if she likes the assignment well enough, she just may pencil in another baby in her leather-bound appointment book.

Gee, how to tell her that she's in for some rude surprises, that children have a way of disrupting even the most carefully laid plans. How to break it to her that being 30-something, all grown up and wise in the ways of the world means absolutely nothing when confronted with a son who has just been stung by a bee or a daughter who has just thrown up in the new Volvo station wagon on the way to the sitter's.

As a matter of fact, the vigor of the 18-year-old mother is a definite advantage when it comes to long, sleepless nights walking the floor with a teething baby. Who has the strength to face a 40th birthday *and* a child who's having a reaction to his DPT shots?

Who wants to be the only silver-haired mother taking her kid to his first day of kindergarten? Will these women be helping their daughters choose their first prom dresses on the same day they apply for Social Security?

Aside from the problem of old age coping with fiery youth, there's the more immediate question of dealing with business pressures while making sure that Junior has his fluoride treatments, gets to his soccer matches and finishes his homework.

Catching a morning commuter flight to L.A. or New York is doubly difficult if daughter's bike tire is flat or she's just broken the bounds of her training bra. Negotiating a union contract at midnight in a hotel room 2,000 miles from home can be complicated by a teen's phone call asking if it's all right to have "a friend" sleep over. My God! What friend?

Frankly, if a "mature" pal of mine were contemplating having a baby while maintaining a career, I'd advise her to forget it. I'd tell her that it's just too tough to be good at both, that even with a helpful husband around the house, the workload would invariably fall on her shoulders, that most days she'd be wrestling with the demons of guilt, wondering if the kids were being ruined by her not being there when they bruised their knees or had to outrun a neighborhood bully. I'd tell her, that in my opinion, the cards are stacked against her.

Yes, as a mother who tried to fashion herself after "June Cleaver" and Donna Reed, that's what I'd tell my hypothetical friend. Except that as I look around, I see a number of women, many without benefit of a well-paid job *or* a husband, punching a clock and raising decent kids at the same time. And no, it's not easy — but no one ever said motherhood was easy — even under the best of circumstances.

Note Space for Mom

34
The Apron

My 21-year-old daughter stood in the middle of her tiny kitchen and looked down at her new dark green dress. "Mom, I need an apron."

I had to sit down; I felt faint. It was the kind of moment mothers live for. She was acknowledging, after all these years, that perhaps my advice had been good.

It was a moment that ought to be captured in marble or at the very least, poetry — so darned satisfying, better than the first step, or "flying up" from Brownies to Girl Scouts. Better even than her high school graduation.

In this case, the subject was just a simple apron, a wisp of cloth, a fragment of fabric, but the big issue was that somewhere along the line she had been listening. Somewhere along the line she had heard me.

All those years when she didn't clean her room, those days when she didn't feed the cat, those nights when she missed curfew by a couple of hours — down deep in the lobes of her brain were messages I thought had been ignored or forgotten.

Like an ancient water torture, my repetitious reminders (she called it nagging) were forever engraved in her consciousness. And like a state-of-the-art computer, she had been able to call up from deep within the system the key phrase: "An apron will protect your clothes."

Now the question is: What kind of apron is suitable? I plan to make it myself. Should it be organdy, lavish with ruffles, or perhaps contemporary blue denim, practical and without frills? Should it be completely businesslike and offer the protection of a butcher's apron, or should it be a simple square of pristine white linen?

Whimsy may not be entirely out of place. I rather liked an apron I saw downtown which said in bold print: "This place is a dump but everyone's friendly."

And when shall I make the presentation? Perhaps a simple ceremony over a frying pan or a double boiler. Obviously, I'll have to give this a lot of thought.

Meanwhile, I'll look forward to life's next shining moment. That will be the rainy day when this same daughter actually wears the waterproof boots I gave her five years ago.

35
Shut Up and Listen

If there's someone who needs a friend, it's the mother who stays at home to raise kids while her smartly dressed neighbors go off to the office or shop. Mom, dressed in jeans and wielding a toilet-bowl brush in one hand and a crying baby in the other, often feels like "The Creature From Another Planet."

These are the times when a kind word, a helping hand or a caring phone call can make all the difference in the world. These are the times when the word "friend" takes on a very special meaning.

A few years ago a number of books came out on the subject of friendship. These tiny tomes were adorned with touching pictures and delicate verse, and while I can be as sentimental and soft as the next woman, I'm more inclined to be tough and demanding when it comes to defining friendship. As you might expect, my views don't easily translate into adorable drawings. For example:

A friend is

. . . someone who'll shut up and listen to your problems even when she thinks her problems are worse.

. . . someone who'll take your kids for the weekend without visibly flinching.

. . . someone who'll love your dog as much as you do.

A friend is someone who will compliment you only when she

means it.

. . .someone who will save her magazines for you without first clipping out the cents-off coupons.

. . .someone who'll save a newspaper article she thinks you will find interesting.

. . .someone who tells you when you're being sarcastic.

. . .someone who won't preach at you about your bad habits.

A friend is someone who'll bring you a small gift now and then for absolutely no reason at all.

. . .someone who'll send you a silly card just to make you smile.

. . .someone who won't give you a surprise party without first telling you about it.

. . .someone who'll buy as many Girl Scout cookies as she can afford in order to help you out.

A friend is someone who'll wait on the phone patiently when your children interrupt.

. . .someone who'll drop in unexpectedly if you like that kind of thing but who won't if you don't.

A friend is someone who doesn't keep track of who entertained whom last.

. . .someone you can call in the middle of the night if you are troubled.

. . .someone who'll like your kids on days when you can't stand them.

. . .someone who'll laugh at your jokes.

. . .someone who's nice to your mother.

. . .someone who isn't perfect ... Just like me.

Note **S**pace for **M**om

Cola

36
Any Port in a Storm

You see them at the supermarket, the women who sluggishly push their over-loaded grocery carts up and down the aisles. You see them at the service station pumping their own gas disconsolately, and you see them at the video rental store, returning films like "Terminator," "Die Hard" and "Lethal Weapon."

It's hard to recognize them as the same vibrant people they were only a few years ago. Zombielike, they seem to have lost their zest for shopping, playing or working. They're the mothers whose grown children have returned to live at home.

As with any other abused segment of the population, there is need for an organization for these women and their husbands. It might be called P.O.R.T. — Parents of Returning Tots.

PORT would provide a place where these people could get together and talk; they'd find they were not alone and that it was not their fault. The problem. they'd soon come to see, is basically financial.

The starry-eyed teenagers who delightedly left home a few years ago have returned because the old homestead provides bed-and-board at the best price in town. The birds who left the nest have come home to roost and the reasons are myriad: a romance gone sour, a college that requires study, or a job that didn't work out.

I pulled the same trick when I was young, moving back home when my young husband was drafted. Earlier, my brother and his bride had lived with my parents at the end of World War II while they saved their earnings to buy a house.

My brother and I shared a trait common to most kids; unless they are unceremoniously kicked out of the house in the first place, it simply never occurs to them that their return may be less than a joyous occasion. They don't realize that the old joke about the folks moving away while the kids are in school is perhaps based in fact.

Thus the need for PORT. PORTers could exchange tips on how to handle the use of the family car, who controls the thermostat, and the sticky question of whether beer and wine are included in the standard room-and-board rate.

PORTers could help each other work out systems on who mows the lawn or cleans the shower now that the "youngsters" are working 40 hours per week. . . If you thought it was tough getting them to do their chores when they were teens, you ain't seen nothin' yet.

Admittedly, most kids will go to other people's homes to eat and sleep if given the opportunity. They make no distinction between soft-hearted middle-aged adults. Clearly, it's any PORT in a storm for them.

A side benefit of PORT membership would be a group rate for group therapy and a psychiatrist who could help them get the word to the kids:

It isn't that we don't love you. It's just that we're a little old to begin having children — *again*.

37
Keeping Cool

It was just your average family birthday party this past Sunday night; only one fire engine and two police cars showed up. That was when the birthday boy's girlfriend fainted dead away on the dance floor due to the heat.

You see, the birthday boy was playing guitar in the band at the time and his date accepted an invitation to dance with another young man. Midway through Rick Springfield's "Don't Talk to Strangers," the young lady literally melted to the floor.

Fortunately, a nurse in a nifty mini-skirt and chain belt was on hand to give first aid, and she instructed that the faintee be placed on a small sofa which was immediately below the bandstand.

The birthday boy's first glimpse of the action was when his girlfriend was carried past him, her pretty summer dress and rhinestone earrings askew. True to the tradition of "the show must go on," he continued playing guitar, executing a pretty nimble solo in the process.

That was when the police arrived — or did the firefighters get there first? It's all a blur in retrospect but apparently the response to the 911 call had been more than adequate.

All things considered, it wasn't a bad day, and certainly as good a birthday celebration as a mother could hope for. You see, after 24 years or parenting, I speak from experience.

Seeing my "baby" hit age 21 recalled other days, other events, and in particular other stand-out years. One particular year lasted *two* years and was spent in Lancaster, Calif. Lancaster, for those of you who don't know it, is located on the high desert north of Los Angeles. It is known for its mild summer days (112 degrees or so), its temperate winters (18 degrees is not uncommon), and the wind that blows relentlessly, piling up sand at the door to a depth of an inch or more.

Our oldest was five when we moved there on a job transfer. The problems seemed to start the minute we hit town. Two of the three children came down with diarrhea while we were staying in a one-bedroom, one-bath apartment at a local motel.

Once we found a house, the pace picked up. I met my first cockroach, got a case of laryngitis, and my husband sprained his ankle. The children had cold after cold until finally one day the baby had to be hospitalized with asthmatic bronchitis.

I was on my way home from visiting the poor little guy in his oxygen tent when an ambulance passed me going in the opposite direction. It turned out that my three-year-old daughter was the passenger/patient, on her way to the hospital because she too was having difficulty breathing.

During the same two years, my husband got a kidney infection, developed an ulcer, and I came down with the mumps. The Chinese exploded their first atomic bomb, a doctor removed a piece of rust from our little girl's eye, and all three kids had tonsillectomies in one day. A week after their surgery, my back went out for the first time and I had to make beds on my hands and knees.

After my bout with German measles, things got better but during those first few years of parenting, I learned to roll with each punch.

That's why, during our recent hot birthday party, I kept my cool.

38
The Pooch Policy

It's official. I received a policy in the mail last week and now our dog, Mr. Spock, is insured for accident and health.

It's a good thing the people in my old neighborhood don't know about it, and if my parents were still alive, they too would be incredulous. I'm still a bit stunned myself. Insurance for a dog? Ridiculous.

Anyone who grew up during the Great Depression knows that if a dog gets sick, it does one of two things. It dies or it gets well. The same goes for an accident — though some soft-hearted souls might have a bone re-set if the recovery seemed fairly uncomplicated.

But I'm not the soft-hearted type. Where I grew up, even a kid didn't get to the doctor's office unless her temperature was over 105. I never even *met* a dentist until I was 12 years old; toothaches were treated with an ice pack and kind words. It's not that my folks were cruel. They simply didn't have the money. When you buy your bread day-old in a big brown bag for five cents, you learn to tolerate a lot of discomfort.

But here I am today, the owner of a pooch who visits the emergency veterinarian hospital if he starts to limp. It was on one such visit that the vet said, "Did you know your dog has a heart murmur?"

I had to laugh. Mr. Spock? Chaser of squirrels, staunch defender against the mailman, the dog who drags me along on walks with the leash pulled so tight that he gasps and chokes the whole distance.

I put off seeing my own vet until guilt got to me and when I took old Spock in, four months later, it was confirmed. He had an enlarged heart. The x-ray and electrocardiogram proved it. That's right. An x-ray and an EKG, and a bill for $90.

I felt rather faint myself but I remembered that in the waiting room I'd seen a brochure about insurance for pets. Like a lamb led to slaughter, I asked about it.

Briefly: Spock could be insured for $69 per year if I bought a three-year policy now. Of course, his heart condition would not be covered for the first six months but since his prognosis was good, it seemed likely that his care later would make this a pretty good investment.

The other nice thing about it was that it allowed me to use the doctor of my choice where the waiting room is beautifully furnished and large enough to eliminate cat and dog fights, and a handy little fire hydrant is just outside the door. Actually, the whole set-up is much more posh than my own doctor's office. I signed on the bottom line.

However, now that I've had a chance to read the small print, I see that Spock is not covered for cosmetic surgery.

I knew there was a catch.

39
Strangeness in the Night

When babies sleep, they sleep almost anywhere. You've seen them slung over shoulders or snoozing in grocery carts. Children of school age are much the same. They may fight going to bed but once there, they collapse into positions of total abandon — a leg hung over the edge of the bed, arms flung over their heads, and they're *gone*.

Teenagers aren't much different. Since most of them finally turn off their lights at 1 a.m., their sleep is that of the dead. Ask any parent who has tried to rouse one of these sleeping giants for school the next morning.

Skipping right through the 20s, that age when sleep seems superfluous to the excitement of living, we get to the middle years where suddenly insomnia raises its ugly head.

Sleeplessness does not discriminate between the sexes. After the 11 o'clock news, the body in its infinite wisdom either lies rigidly in bed, eyes staring into the darkness, or inexplicably drifts right off to peaceful slumber only to come awake with a start at 3 a.m.

Then the mind takes over. Like a computer whose power supply is shorting out, random weird thoughts move sporadically through the consciousness: Is it your turn to drive tomorrow or did you switch last week? Is your dog whining or is it the neighbor's? Was that an earthquake or someone opening the front door?

You turn over on your side and it's on to bigger things: Is your job secure? Are the kids headed for trouble? Will the company make it through the recession? Will you need to replace the roof this year? Is college for all the kids going to be affordable and is it even a good idea?

Sleep continues to elude you and the thoughts grow ever heavier: Is nuclear war inescapable? Are you fulfilling your role on this earth or just taking up space? What's it all about, Alfie?

The thoughts you've repressed all day, the fears that were held at bay while you grocery-shopped or commuted home float about the room like faceless phantoms. The tiny nightlight in the hallway seems as bright as a strobe. It penetrates eyelids that are suddenly too thin.

Finally, in desperation, you get out of bed ever so carefully so as not to wake your mate. You slip your toes into the scuffed slippers you keep meaning to replace and throw on the robe that was a gift but never your color, and you tiptoe out to the kitchen.

It's ablaze with light; the dog sleeping in his chair opens one eye to see what all the commotion is about. The smell of frying eggs and toasting bread assails your nostrils and you realize that your musician son has just gotten home. He's wide awake, hungry and eager to talk.

You manage only an affectionate pat on his arm and stumble to the sink, toss down an antihistamine tablet to control the hay fever that seems rougher at night. Not incidentally, you're looking for those promised sleep-inducing side effects.

A stop at the bathroom to insure a few hours of uninterrupted rest, a glimpse in the merciless mirror, then back to bed, and after a half-hour of tossing, you finally drift off.

Moments later, your sleeping mate suddenly comes awake, stares into the darkness, and repeats the whole routine, step for step, like a carefully choreographed ballet of the night.

40
The Incredible Shrinking Woman

I've just been through a multi-faceted physical examination where one is poked, prodded and weighed. Blood is extracted and sampled for disease and deterioration. Wires are attached to the body in order that an electrocardiogram can determine if, indeed, the heart has ever truly been broken.

Liquid bodily wastes are labeled and scrutinized in much the same way a vintner might judge his fall harvest. One can almost imagine a technician proclaiming the vintage as "amusing but lacking in bouquet and body."

The eyes are checked for symptoms of glaucoma and the hearing is tested by a series of space-age sounds. A technician wraps one's arm tightly and watches as small gauges measure the pressure of the blood.

Prior to such an exam, it is important not to eat anything, My fast lasted 14 hours, an unheard of period of time for me to go hungry.

After all this prodding into the temple of my soul, I came home thankful to have the chore behind me for another year. My son greeted me and asked, "How did it go, Mom?"

I'm sure he was hoping for a brief, cheerful response. I looked at him sadly and slowly replied, "I've shrunk another quarter of an inch."

He had the nerve to laugh!

"What about your blood pressure? What about those times when you get shaky and tired?"

I had forgotten to ask.

The nurse had put me on the scale and as she wrote down the vital statistics, I had asked, "How tall am I?"

"Five feet, six inches."

She had no way of knowing she was turning a knife in my heart. I've *always* been five-feet-seven. It has said so on my driver's license for more than 30 years. I was always a forward in the girl's basketball games in P.E., the one who stood in the back line in Girls' Chorus, and the one who could reach things on the top kitchen shelf.

I've been proud of my height and always stood up straight without reminders from my mother. In three-inch heels I've been able to intimidate willful clerks and until a few years ago command the respect of my children simply because I was bigger than they were.

That's all changed now.

Somehow I lost one-fourth of an inch, then last year a half-inch more, and this time, though I stretched with all my might, the best I could do was five-feet-six.

"The Incredible Shrinking Woman, that's me," I sobbed hysterically to my son.

"That's OK, Mom; we love you anyway," he reassured me from his lofty six feet.

I just wish he hadn't patted me on the top of the head.

41
Merry, Merry

It's Christmas Eve and in schools and churches across the country, the season of the Christmas play is just about over. Those adults who volunteered their directorial skills, those children who offered their services as shepherd boys, tin soldiers and sugar plums are about to take their final bows.

Sewing machines that turned nylon tulle into fairy wings and green felt into elfin shoes have quieted. Paint brushes that transformed a dull schoolroom stage into Santa's sparkling workshop lay forgotten, congealed into an unredeemable mass.

For me it means that after a month of waking in the night in cold sweats, I can finally relax and know that no one is going to come looking for me. Because, like a veteran of some momentous battle, I still have flashbacks to the time when I was 10 years old and I got involved in the Sunday school play.

One thing is sure: I must have been drafted; I never would have volunteered. I don't even remember now what part I was to play, but with each rehearsal I showed up more reluctantly until finally, on the day before the pageant, I realized I could never memorize my lines, I retreated under my bed and could not be bribed or dragged out.

Apparently the show went on without me. The star rose in the east, the shepherds kept their flocks, the wise men found their way — and my future as an actress went right down the tubes.

At any rate, I have the greatest respect for the people who put together the traditional Christmas play, the teachers who stand in the wings mouthing lines to children paralyzed with fright, the band instructors who with only a drum and a triangle can produce a memorable "Little Drummer Boy."

I'm in awe of the choral conductor who can take 50 voices ranging from childish soprano to hearty bass, and produce near-harmony out of chaos. I'm profoundly grateful for the drama coaches who must round up props as well as missing actors, break up backstage clinches and give up lunch-hours for an event to which some parents must be dragged.

I trust that after tomorrow they will all take a well-deserved rest and I wish them the merriest of Christmases.

Note Space for Mom

42
An Apocryphal Tale?

The following may be true or it may be simply an apocryphal tale but parents everywhere would be wise to heed it. It seems that on Thanskgiving Day last year a woman was injured and severely traumatized as she attempted to serve her holiday dinner.

Word has it that she was struck in the eye by a tomato aspic thrown by her 10-year-old son. She also suffered contusions when her 12-year-old daughter angrily threw down a loaf of hard French bread; it bounced and hit the woman's arm.

Apparently, the mother had tried to vary her menu for Thanksgiving dinner. It seems safe to say that her efforts were not successful. Sketchy accounts report that Mom had served the usual turkey and stuffing, olives and bread-and-butter pickles, candied yams and mashed potatoes, but she had omitted the traditional fruit gelatin and Parker House rolls. Bored by years of cooking the same thing, she had tried to make dinner a little more interesting with a tomato aspic and French bread.

While my heart goes out to this unidentified woman, I think she should have known better. She should have known that you just don't alter holiday traditions that have been established in families for years. Children will simply not stand for it.

Children are tyrants — as crotchety and hide-bound as little old men when it comes to changing their ways. For example, have you ever announced to the kids that this year you will go to Grandma's house instead of Grandma coming to yours? Have you ever tried to serve breakfast *before* opening the Christmas stockings? Have you ever changed Christmas dinner from 2 p.m. to 5 p.m.?

Don't be silly. Your life wouldn't be worth a plugged nickel.

Kids won't let you put an angel on the top of the tree if you've always put a star there before. They won't let you buy a spruce if you've always had a pine, and they certainly will not let you experiment with a white tree trimmed in blue if they've always had a green tree with multi-colored lights and ornaments.

Thus, it certainly should come as no surprise that one does not mess with the usual holiday menu. If you long for a lemon pie on Thankgiving but the children have always had pumpkin-with-whipped-cream, forget it.

ON THE OTHER HAND, as children reach their teens, the rules of the game may suddenly change but all of the players will not be notified.

"Oh, Mom, do we *have* to sing carols on Christmas Eve? It's so cornball," says daughter, and "Uh, Dad, I won't be going with you to pick out a tree, not if we have to take the old blue station wagon," says son. (Teens are allergic to stations wagons.)

When my college-age daughter announced via long distance that she had become a vegetarian and would only eat seafood for holiday dinners, I was caught with a 20-pound turkey in the freezer.

"We can still have stuffing and pickles and pies," she told me cheerily, "but maybe we can have shrimp."

I hung up wondering how you stuff a shrimp . . . and where?

It often gets worse as the kids hit their 20s. They are bored easily by their parents and disdain the same old get-togethers of family and friends. They frequently accept invitations from school chums or casual acquaintances to go elsewhere for the holidays, and they're very cavalier about the fact that you were sort of counting on them.

Smart parents, however, will view this as the long-awaited freedom from the kiddies' domination of the holidays; some may even plan a trip to Hawaii. But, just as they're packing their bags and humming "Lovely Hula Hands," the phone will ring and a kid will have news:

"My girlfriend can't go to Aspen after all, so I figured I'd just come home for Christmas."Then it's decision time. Do the folks cut the cord, tell the kid they're sorry but they've made travel plans? Or do they shrug their shoulders, adjust their calendar and feign enthusiasm: "That's great. You know where we live . . ."

If so, it's then time to get out the trusty old "Joy of Cooking" and look under "T" for traditional. . .And maybe "S" for shrimp.

Note Space for Mom

43
Bottled Water in Her Veins

If you've ever fretted over a child's first walk alone to the grocery store or his first trip to the movies without you, you'll understand — a little — how it is to have a grown daughter who is a world traveler.

I don't know how I ever spawned a creature who would travel on a dusty bus through the wilds of Mexico, sleep on the beaches of Greece or take a night train through France to an unknown destination. *I* have a hard time driving 50 miles to San Jose but she is ready at the drop of a hat to head for San Jose — San Jose, Costa Rica!

Maybe it has something to do with the fact that I wouldn't let her ride her bike in the street until she was 8, but the kid has bottled water in her veins and carries her passport handy the way other people carry their driver's license.

During her absences, the mail has been mercifully slow, so much so that by the time I receive word of her adventures, they are history. Otherwise, you can imagine my panic had I known that on one occasion she'd been lost on a crowded Spanish beach, wearing only a bikini and unable to find her friends, clothes or purse.

How would I have felt if I had known that during her first month in Mexico she became dreadfully ill but was rescued by a new male acquaintance who bought some nausea pills at the *farmacia* and encouraged her to wash them down with three pina coladas?

Could I have enjoyed Christmas knowing she was sharing it with two other lonely females in a Madrid version of a greasy spoon? Or that she had lived for days in Paris on apples and bread but still found it exhilarating to climb the Eiffel Tower or stroll the banks of the Seine.

Would this past Thanksgiving have been so relaxed for me if I had known she was by herself in a rented room in Mexico City, lonely but pleased with herself for surviving the day?

Could I even imagine the wonder she felt at visiting Paraiso Escondido (Lost Paradise), many miles out of Acapulco, where there was no potable water and where for several days she ate only fresh fish, rice and Coca Cola — three times a day! There she slept in a hammock in a thatched hut and swam in a black lagoon when the heat became unbearable.

Wonder of wonders, she came home this week. She's enjoying the electric blanket, the microwave oven and the luxury of a leisurely bath. But I know that in a month or so the wanderlust will overtake her and I'll feel just like I did when she was a little girl striking out for the grocery store all by herself: worried sick.

44
Painful Gramps

One of the pleasures of the 1984 Summer Olympics was the United Airlines commercials which featured men and women well over the age of 55 in various athletic pursuits. They looked like real people, not a New York ad agency's svelte parody of senior citizens.

A plump woman in a skirted swimsuit, noseclip and bathing cap in place, taking a belly flop into a pool; a heavyset gentleman lifting a trunk while imagining himself an Olympic weight-lifter; and two very senior skaters twirling gently on the ice to a Sarajevo finale and a warm hug. These people looked like the grandparents we all wish we'd had.

Perhaps closer to reality were the older folks I encountered at the mall the other day. I had just sat down with a cup of coffee to rest and recuperate from some serious shopping, and to do some people-watching from the little "sidewalk cafe," when voices boomed from behind me.

"Kids these days! They don't want to *work* for anything. They want it all handed to them," said one man. The couple at the other table chuckled and nodded in agreement.

I twisted ever so discreetly in my chair to get a better look at the speakers. Two couples sat at adjoining tables. They had evidently just struck up a conversation. All were in their 60s — friendly, portly, middle class.

The same man continued: "My brother's kid came home from college with long hair and a beard, and my brother told him to get a haircut and a shave — or move out."

"What happened?" asked the other man.

"He cut his hair," laughed the first, "and he's a real good kid now."

I felt a little shudder go up my spine.

"I have a niece, "continued the first man, "who got a degree at Stanford, got married and moved out to the country. They're *farming*," he said incredulously. "She and her husband don't even have indoor plumbing.

"I told them I'm not coming to see them in a place like that." His last statement seemed to indicate that it "served them right" that old Unc' wouldn't come for a visit, but I was still trying to reconcile the Stanford niece with the aforementioned "kids who want it all handed to them."

The book, "I'm OK, You're OK" came to mind. I remembered the author's "child, adult, parent" theory in which the "parent" personality hands down pronouncements of "truth" without regard to the realities of the situation.

The generalities were now flying thick and fast between the two couples. "Kids," it seemed were sure a pain in the neck. They either "never come to see you," or "never leave home." The little ones "are into everything when they come to visit" and "if you want pretty things in your home, you can't have them if you have grandchildren."

I was feeling sorry for any young adults related to these people when the first man said, "We never had any kids — and we're glad now that we didn't."

The other couple looked surprised, as if they'd been playing a game with unauthorized players.

"Yeah," said the first man more softly. "Sometimes we miss having them . . ."

45
Gee, Thanks but No Thanks

Whether it's Mothers Day, Christmas or her birthday, most kids have a problem with what to give Mom. Here are some tips on what NOT to give *this* Mom:

Please, no exotic house plants. It's like giving me another child to care for, without consulting me on the adoption. Sure, a nice green number that thrives on drought and indifference might be OK, but don't saddle me with something that requires "light misting daily" or must be put into a closet each night in order to set blossoms.

Please don't give me any furry little kittens who hide under the bed when I'm late for an appointment, nor any warm soft puppies who piddle in puddles in the middle of the living room carpet. I've been through 2 a.m. feedings and walking babies back to sleep; I don't need any more infants, including the four-footed variety.

Also, I'd just as soon you didn't give me any of the perfumes or colognes that are heavily advertised on TV. One in particular stands out: the woman who pulls off her apron, lets down her hair, unbuttons the top button on her blouse and wets her lips. Really, it's all I can do to get supper on the table for a hungry horde. I can't cope with a crazed animal nibbling on my ear at 6 p.m.

Thanks awfully but please, no super jumbo cosmetic kits

featuring lavender eyeliner, purple blush and peach mascara. I don't have time to contour my face with earth colors; I'll just suck in my cheeks for special occasions.

Dearest ones, I truly loved the little clay plaques with the tiny hands pressed into them, and the slightly crooked ceramic ash trays glazed in bright green and red. Now that you're older, I know you're still looking for an inexpensive way out, but the "coupon book" has its drawbacks. Sure, it's handmade and cute as all get-out, full of "good fors" such as "Good for one free car wash," "Good for one complete housecleaning," "Good for one free kitchen clean-up."

I've tried to collect on these coupon offers but my timing must be off. The sweet considerate gift-giver disappears and in his place I find a surly, surprised kid who hasn't the foggiest memory of what I'm talking about when I wake him on Saturday morning and try to collect my "gift."

"What's that scrap of paper you're waving in my face, Mom?" he mumbles, and rolls over and back to sleep while I go wash the car myself.

Another thing, kids. It took me a long time to get used to the idea of my daughters having pierced ears, and even longer for my son's, but please, I really don't want to have my ears pierced, even if you're willing to pay for it. I am not now nor will I ever be "hip," and anyhow, I've always thought that if the good Lord had wanted me to have another orifice in my head, he would have done the job himself.

As for breakfast in bed, thanks but no thanks. I'm sure it would be delicious, fun, and a real novelty, but I prefer to grope my way to the kitchen and enjoy my corn flakes and coffee in relative solitude. If you want to make me really happy, just sleep in and let me read the paper by myself.

When it comes to traditional gifts, I know I've often requested that you not buy me chocolates. Do me a favor; ignore it. Better yet, take me directly to the candy store where I can choose my favorites. Somehow, when you do the buying I usually end up with nuts and chews, *your* favorites, and then I must open the box immediately or risk being boycotted on my next birthday.

One thing I will happily accept for any occasion is a hug, a phone call or a note. While I may not want to be showered with gifts, I certainly don't mind being drenched with affection.

Note Space for Mom

46
The Mystery of Sisterhood

The daughter of a friend of mine came to town to visit recently. She brought her two adorable little girls, Sarah, 21 months, and Morgan, seven months. I immediately went over to see the children to enjoy vicariously the pleasures of grand-motherhood.

Morgan lay in her grandma's crib, wearing only a diaper. When she didn't have her toes stuck in her mouth, she was gurgling, cooing and entertaining for all she was worth, the very epitome of Babydom. The older, more reserved Sarah looked on from the safety of her aunt's arms at all the excitement her little sister was generating.

Sarah then expressed a desire to get into the crib with Morgan and this she did, whereupon she affectionately patted Morgan on the head *and stepped on Morgan's hand* — all at the same time.

It was a scene encapsulating the complexities of sisterhood, that love-hate relationship that will bond — and separate — Morgan and Sarah all their lives.

I speak from experience. I am a sister, and I have two daughters who are (obviously) sisters.

My own sister was 4½ years old when I was born and from the start she had absolutely no use for me. That didn't change until she was an adult. I know because she *told* me, much later on. I, on the other hand, having no idea how she felt about me, admired and looked up to her as the wiser older sister.

She now admits to me that later on I was more than just a pest. She was worried that I might steal her boyfriends, though I fail to see how a clumsy 11-year-old could steal anything from a smart, pretty 15-year-old. Her insecurities stemmed, apparently, from the time of my birth when I usurped her favored position with an older brother. He abruptly stopped paying attention to her and started paying attention to me, and in those days there were no books by experts to point out the possible problem for our parents.

So here I was, this baby kid, totally innocent of any evil intent, and my sister loathed me.

Things got off to a smoother start with my own two daughters. The first girl was 19 months old when the second one came along. Number One was asleep the day I brought Number Two home from the hospital. When Number Two went to sleep, Number One woke up. It seemed to continue that way for a long time and thus Number One was not terribly pushed out of shape by the demands of the new houseguest.

When my son was born 22 months later, the two girls had each other for company. They never missed a beat when their brother moved in, and their friendship was strong well into their teens.

Then, inevitably, we were into the comparisons, jealousies, competition and more than a few screaming matches, but underneath was a strong affection that visitors to the household never failed to notice.

The intricacies of the girl's relationship still delights and dismays me at times, and is a source of wonder and confusion to their brother who is not, and never can be, a sister.

All of this tumbled through my mind as I witnessed the Sarah-and-Morgan tableau and Sarah's seemingly casual attempt to maim her baby sister. I almost voiced it to their young mother, but she had other problems on her mind — like how to get them both down for a nap at the same time so that she herself could get some rest.

How to tell her that there is no rest for the mother of sisters?

Note Space for Mom

47
A Fragile Thread

My barking dog woke me first. Then I heard the knocking on the door and the phone ringing in the kitchen. My husband grabbed his robe while I picked up the bedroom extension.

A neigbor's voice at the door was saying, "Your son's been in an accident" at the same moment my son was saying in my ear, "Mom, can you and Dad come get us? Someone ran into my car. We're in Fremont."

When rousted from sleep at 2 a.m., the brain comes jerkily awake and the heart pounds furiously, but thank God I knew almost instantly that everything was basically OK, that we simply had another family crisis on our hands, not a major tragedy. We hadn't heard the phone when David tried to call us the first time so he had called our neighbor.

Within five minutes we were in action: a call to the towing service, another call back to David who was standing at a pay phone in the icy pre-dawn with his two friends. My husband was out the door and on his way. Wide-eyed by now, I made myself a cup of tea, dragged out the sewing machine and hemmed a dress for a friend. Anything to keep the hands and mind busy.

At 5 a.m. a tired group walked in the door — my son, his friends, my husband, and the tow-truck driver who took me up on the offer of a cup of coffee and proceeded to shoot the breeze for half an hour. Finally, with the aid of some not-so-subtle hints, the kaffee-klatsch broke up and the family went to bed. My son's little 1967 Mustang sat out front, crumpled into what is known in the insurance business as a "total," a victim of a hit-and-run driver.

The next days were interesting. I learned that David had been sitting at a stop light when he was hit, that a witness — a 30ish woman with *purple hair* — had seen the accident and had pursued and caught up with the errant driver. She got his license number and convinced him to turn around and follow her back to the scene.

"Don't turn me in," he had pleaded in what she sensed to be a drunken manner. "I don't have a license." He was a mature man, not a teenager.

He followed the lady with the purple hair for a short distance but then veered off and disappeared into the night, not a terribly smart move on his part since he'd left quite a bit of his car at the scene of the accident and she had his license number.

The Fremont police officer who responded to the call was more than courteous to my long-haired musician son and his companions. His phone calls over the next few days were prompt and helpful. Since he worked the graveyard shift, most of our conversations took place at odd hours like 11 p.m. and 6:30 a.m.

I also found it educational that unlike TV's cops, the police politely waited for the hit-and-run driver to turn himself in, even though they could have easily found him.

"I'm going to have to call again and tell him it's extremely important for him to come in," the officer told me, a remark that might be considered carrying courtesy too far.

The driver finally did come forward and the purple-haired lady identified him. He was a salesman for a new-car dealership and he'd been driving a company car.

The whole incident is what you might call "an open and shut case," except that now my son has no car, he and his friends have some minor doctor bills to pay, and there's the little matter of the $111 towing charge from Fremont.

Just your typical Saturday night happening except that it served as a valuable reminder that life hangs by a very fragile thread — and we were luckier than many.

STAFF

48
Gathering the Brood

You'd think I'd remember what vacations were like when the kids were little. You'd think I'd welcome the fact that the children are now grown and it's no longer my responsibility to provide them with summer fun.

You might also think that my husband and I would relish the idea of being alone after all those years of sharing, that we'd run off and leave no address or phone number.

You'd think all of that if you were unswervingly logical, but I'm too much a mother to be logical. Some masochistic urge drives me to try to bring my little brood together, and this year a very kind friend provided the perfect spot — a wonderful condominium at Lake Tahoe.

We all arrived at Tahoe from various points and hugged each other in greeting; familial affection oozed from every pore. It looked like we'd have a wonderful time but old habits die hard, and despite the fact that all the kids were capable of entertaining themselves, I immediately went into my camp-counselor role.

"We will assemble in the living room at 9 tomorrow morning and go into town for breakfast," I informed them. "Afterwards, you are free to pursue your own interests until lunch at 2 p.m., to be followed by swimming and sunning.

"Plan to be dressed and ready for dinner at 8 p.m.; we'll take two cars so that those who wish to visit the casinos may do so and those who wish to come back early will have that option."

They were all remarkably agreeable to the schedule but their enthusiastic cooperation at cleaning up for dinner left my husband and me with no hot water for showers.

Other little problems developed and things began to unravel after several days of togetherness. Tempers grew visibly shorter and familiar patterns of sibling behavior surfaced. A wisecrack about our vegetarian family member led to a retort about eating "red flesh" that served to put a definite damper on the prime-rib buffet at Harrah's.

One kid's effortless win of $90 at the gaming table was viewed suspiciously by another who had painfully lost $20 in nickels at the slot machines.

My "Morning Activities Report" was cut short the next day when the big winner announced she was going shopping with her winnings. Someone else peeled off to go sight-seeing. My older daughter gently explained to me that it is often difficult to organize so many very different adults. I nodded sadly, realizing I was now a mother with no one to mother.

Happily, there was no bloodshed the rest of the week and when the kids finally took off, my husband and I looked forward to one last day alone. We had just returned to the condo from the airport when suddenly we heard a key turn in the lock. Five strangers and a cocker spaniel walked in!

It seems there had been a small misunderstanding; our generous friend had inadvertently loaned us the condo while at the same time her real estate agent had rented it to someone else. After confirming the situation by phone, we asked for 45 minutes to clean up and clear out. Like a speeded-up Laurel-and Hardy, we whirled through the house, finished and headed down Highway 50 for home.

We weren't upset, we weren't distraught, and we certainly weren't surprised. Family vacations never seem to turn out the way you thought they would.

49
The Bride Wore White

The wedding was scheduled for 1 p.m. but the bride-to-be was still out at 11 shopping for a slip. Her family arrived at the apartment just as she rushed in, breathless from her search at three stores for a petticoat that just met the hem of her ankle-length wedding gown.

Yes, the dress was white and extremely demure. A few wedding guests might snicker but it suited her perfectly: sheer cotton with long full sleeves, a nipped-in waist and a high stand-up collar. It made the bride's very short, contemporary hair style look almost Victorian, as if the curls on top had been piled there in a gesture to the 1890s. An antique pin borrowed from her mother and worn at the throat completed the look.

The bride hurriedly dressed in the bedroom as the groom, attired in a handsome beige suit, served coffee and sweet rolls to his future in-laws. The brother of the bride snapped a few pictures. It was all very relaxed.

Outside, the October day in Santa Cruz was sunny and clear with a taste of the sea, perfect for an outdoor ceremony at The Farm, a restaurant and collection of shops in nearby Soquel.

The minister had been recruited only two weeks before, a hospital chaplain recommended by a friend. The groom had forgotten to choose a reading for the exchange of vows but he seemed unconcerned, confident the minister would come through.

At 12:30 the bride and groom got in their car and drove to The Farm. Relatives and friends were arriving and walking down the path from their cars. The happy couple greeted them, making introductions and obviously enjoying the party atmosphere. No last-minute jitters with the bride locked away out of sight, no groom pacing nervously in an ante-room. No practical jokers writing ribald comments in shaving cream on the windows of the get-away car. Harp music filled the warm air.

The minister took his place at the top of the grassy clearing. The best man and the maid of honor stepped forward, followed by the bride and groom, side by side. The bride's father, who in another era might have "given the bride away," smiled. His wife dabbed happily at tears.

The words were brief, non-denominational but sweetly sentimental and charming. Rings were exchanged; gold glinted in the sun. They kissed.

The ceremony over, the crowd strolled a few yards to the terrace for refreshments and champagne. The three-tiered cake was cut, the bridal bouquet tossed, and finally, the blue garter thrown — the blue garter the bride had just bought that morning, caught up finally in traditions she had steadfastly ignored for the past five years.

Off to one side an uncle whispered to the bride's mother: "Why did they decide to get married?"

"Because they were ready to make the commitment," she replied, obviously very pleased — and more than a little relieved.

50
Did a Nurse Switch Babies?

I have a married daughter who buys groceries only when she gets hungry. She says it saves money and also helps her to stay slim. When I hear her say things like that, I think that maybe a careless nurse must have switched babies on me. No daughter of mine would willingly live with an empty cupboard and bare refrigerator.

The only other possible explanation is some kind of genetic mix-up where the X chromosome and the Y chromosome repressed the F (for Food) chromosome. Otherwise, my usually sensible daughter would have a kitchen like mine, double-stocked with all kinds of "back-up" containers of peanut butter, catsup and pickle relish.

Because of my peculiar obsession with never running out of food, there is a well-marked trail where my car leaves the house at least every other day and drives to the grocery store for some commodity without which we could not get through another day. Today it was lunchmeat. I don't even *eat* lunchmeat!

You'll have to forgive me. I get a little testy in December. It's the month of making grocery lists which are longer than the letters I write my sister.

I wake up in a cold sweat each morning, muttering things like "walnuts, unsalted sweet butter, mince meat." I sit bolt-upright and grab the pad on my night-table and start scribbling:

"yams, celery, artichoke hearts." I run to the kitchen and throw a piece of frozen bread in the toaster and write across the little paper wrapper that enclosed my tea bag: "Order rurkey!!!"

I'm near hysteria and my family doesn't even seem to notice. They do, however, walk in wide circles around me and when they think I'm not looking, they grab my grocery list and write something ridiculous on it like "milk, cereal, bread," things I forgot to buy on my last frantic trip to the store.

I clip recipes like mad and promise myself that this year I really will make a cranberry salad that's edible. I keep trying for just the right combination, but I note with some pride that my mother stubbornly made tomato aspic every Christmas despite the fact the whole family hated it.

I rummage through my tattered Betty Crocker cookbook in search of my favorite stuffing recipe. The pages crumble and fall to the floor, a little snowfall around my feet. I gather them up and tape them together. I would *never* trust my stuffing to a Johnny-Come-Lately like Julia Child.

In preparation for my major grocery-shopping foray, I clean out the freezer and find a $10 package of frozen shrimp which I purchased last Christmas Eve. I scrutinize them carefully and reluctantly throw them out.

In the bathroom, I stop in the middle of putting on my makeup and write across the nearest facial tissue: "choc. chips, brandy, half-and-half." On my way to work, I stop at a red light and grope around in the glove compartment. My hand finds the auto owner's manual. I pull it out and write on the cover: "green onions, cookie sprinkles, white wine."

The last item reminds me that the only thing in my daughter's freezer compartment is half a dozen chilled champagne glasses. I add a note to my list:

"Check hospital records for Oct. 16, 1960."

51
The Groupie

You have every right to ask. What *was* I doing in a bar at 1 a.m. listening to rock and roll music? Am I not a pillar of respectability, the virtuous mother of three, a former parents' club president?

Didn't I once teach Sunday school, abhor mini-skirts and favor Neil Diamond? So what was I doing in this place, planted on a barstool, clapping my hands to "Let's Get Physical!"?

The crowd around me didn't seem to notice that I was out of place. They were all moving to the beat, sweat pouring down their faces as they jockeyed to stay on the tiny dance floor. "She's a *man*-eater," wailed the girl singer.

My partner pulled me into the sea of gyrating forms and I was immediately swallowed up. The pulsating rhythm found its way into my bloodstream and my involuntary nervous system took over my hands and feet.

"Hit Me With Your Best Shot," implored the bass player, and the woman behind me threw her hip into mine, hard enough to knock me down but there was no room to fall. "Ummmmphhh!" I gasped.

I was impervious to pain at this point; my mind was on other things, my eyes glued to the lead guitarist of the band. Six feet tall, slim to the point of reediness, he was hermetically sealed in black spandex pants. A traditional white dress-shirt was loosely buttoned and accented with a skinny black-and-turquoise tie.

His brown hair was cut fairly short for a rock-and-roller, and his strong jawline seemed in contrast to a nose that could only be described as "cute." A sensuous mouth seemed contorted in pain as he leaned backwards, pulling each note from the gut of his jet-black quitar.

By now my dancing partner was aware that my attention was elsewhere. My gaze went past his shoulder, my eyes magnetically drawn again and again to the guitarist.

Is this what a "groupie" feels like? I wondered. Is this what the mystique of rock is all about? Is this why religious groups consistently condemn the music of the younger generation? I had no desire to examine such questions. I was caught in an emotional attraction over which I had no control.

The spell was broken when the group announced a short break. I returned to my barstool and carried on a trivial conversation for 15 minutes. I can't remember now what I talked about; my mind was only on that guitarist, my eye on the clock.

Then the band leaped back on stage and the energy returned. I was the first one out on the dance floor, pulling my partner behind me in order to secure a place close to the bandstand.

The thumping beat of "The Eye of the Tiger" consumed the crowd. I threw myself into the dance, trying to catch the attention of the guitarist, but he was absorbed, his eyes closed and his body bent as he first caressed, then assaulted his guitar.

"Heck," I thought, "I can remember when *I* was the most important thing in his life. I can remember when he used to sit on my lap and let me read to him from Richard Scarry's 'Best Word Book Ever.'"

The band broke into "Turn Me Loose," then moved into "I'm in Love With the Other Woman." Suddenly the guitarist looked up, grinned at me and silently mouthed, "Hi, Mom."

52
Mother of the Bride

Now that it's June, the traditional month of weddings, I realize that some of my friends still aren't speaking to me because I got off so easy when my daughter got married last fall.

Because the bride and groom had lived together in another city for about five years, they handled all the arrangements themselves: securing the location, sending the invitations, choosing the music, ordering the flowers and planning for the refreshments and cake.

I didn't have to lift a finger except to stop on my way to the wedding and pick up the bouquets and boutonnieres. I felt like a guest except that I was privileged to arrive early and help the bride dress, but that too was more a symbol than a necessity.

Naturally, given the choice, I probably would have opted for a more traditional arrangement, but having dealt so long with the problem of how to identify my daughter's live-in boyfriend, I kind of felt they owed me one. Besides, I long ago learned that life doesn't always follow the script.

So on that October day I was able to relax and enjoy the occasion with none of the stress that is the usual accompaniment for the mother of the bride. Eight months later I am still grateful as I observe what's going on in some of my friends' lives.

For instance, one friend's daughter just got married in Southern California in a megabuck production which included a designer gown and a sit-down dinner for hundreds at a club in Malibu.

What should have been a perfect occasion turned into chaos when a guest's baby went into convulsions and turned blue. Paramedics and a fire engine arrived on the scene but I'm sure my friend's good manners and compassion prevented her from saying anything unkind to the distressed young mother who knew beforehand that the baby was ill and who had disregarded a basic rule of etiquette: Babies are not welcome guests at weddings — unless they belong to the bride and groom.

Happily, the child was soon OK but only an hour later the paramedics and fire engine returned to the same reception to attend a man who had collapsed on the dance floor. Fearing he was in shock, someone grabbed a tablecloth to wrap around him, ignoring the fact that the cloth was on a table set with crystal and china. The gentleman recovered. The table settings did not.

Closer to home, I saw a young woman go right through the ceiling when she found out her mother had mailed the wedding invitations without enough postage. Fortunately, the post office either slipped up or chose to look the other way when the telltale envelopes with the outdated "LOVE" postage stamps made their way through the postal process. The invitations arrived without the embarrasing "postage due" message stamped across their fronts.

At my own wedding, remembered through the mists of time, my mother-in-law-to-be did the floral arrangements only to have one large gladioli-filled vase topple over into the center aisle only moments before the procession. And the fruit punch, ordered by *my* mother and delivered to the church's reception hall still frozen, didn't thaw in time. With nothing to pour, Mom was chipping off chunks of punch and putting them into the guests' cups.

No question about it: I'm still grateful that last October my position as Mother of the Bride was strictly an honorary title.

Note Space for Mom

ONLY 45 MORE
SHOPPING DAYS
TIL CHRISTMAS!

53
The November Blahs

Here it is only the first week in November and the Christmas displays are already dusty. If that hasn't dampened your attitude about the upcoming festivities, then I'm here to help.

Why wait for holiday depression to sneak up on you: Start now to consider the complications that await you, the shopping that will have you lying awake at night, the chores that will keep you busy until well past midnight on December 24th.

My own approach has been to ignore it. Coward that I am, I hadn't even faced decisions about Thanksgiving. Mercifully, my daughter came through with her usual invitation to join them for a vegetarian meal, and I jumped on it like a dog on a bar of tofu. So what does it matter that I haven't had a Thanksgiving turkey for four years? It's a small price to pay for only having to provide dessert.

Last year I picked up frozen pies from the supermarket just hours before they were to be served. Did I feel guilty about it? Do chickens have beaks? As a matter of fact, Mrs. Smith's pies did just fine, thank you, and as everyone sat around, stuffed to the gills with wok-fried shrimp, it was really of little interest whether the pumpkin and mince were Mrs. Smith's or Mrs. Borgman's.

Americans worship food too much anyhow. Most mothers don't have time to even *think* about what they're thankful for;

they're too busy making stuffing. And while Mom is cutting and chopping like a woman possessed, the kids are into the olives, pickles and stuffed dates. When called to the groaning board, they're already groaning themselves.

That explains why my personal heroine is the woman I know who roasts a turkey a day or so before Thanksgiving, then serves the family turkey sandwiches on the big day "because that's what they're really interested in anyhow."

Besides, where is there a refrigerator actually large enough to accommodate the tons of food left over from a grand-scale Thanksgiving dinner? Did you ever notice that women's magazines only show you the table set with the bird, cranberries, squash, rolls, pies, etc.? They never show you the poor housewife later that night, inextricably wound in yards of Saran Wrap, trying to find a place for leftovers.

Thanksgiving, however, is small potatoes (sorry) when compared to the Decamber holidays. Food is just the tip of the iceberg at the winter solstice. They key word here is "expectation". It's a heavy responsibility making dreams come true. Then too, gathering all the family for the holidays ain't all it's cracked up to be when Grandma and Grandpa have divorced and remarried, when Dad's son by a former marriage (the bed wetter!) is coming to visit, and 14 people will be sharing two baths. Maybe snow falling outside would make it better but I doubt it.

No, you'll just have to figure out a holiday schedule in which you can see everyone you're obligated to see, cook enough food to feed everyone you're obligated to feed, and wield that charge card 'til the numbers fall off.

I can see I've ruined your day, haven't I? Well, go ahead; be the first kid on your block to have Holiday Depression. Have a good cry, and when you're done, maybe it will all come back to you — the real meaning of those December holidays.

54
Deja Vu in the Checkout Line

I was standing in line at the cash register, buying those last-minute items for Christmas — wrapping paper, ribbon and Tylenol — when I saw her. She looked to be in her early 30s, attractive but tired looking. One of her hands was locked firmly on a five-year-old's arm. The other gripped the shopping cart in which two toddlers, knee-deep in Playskool and Tinker Toys, were locked in mortal combat.

I kept an eye on her as she checked out, and saw her go to a small station wagon in the parking lot where she proceeded to buckle the little ones firmly into their car seats, round up the five-year-old who had wandered off to look at a bird, and lift all the bags from the cart to the car. She then drove off carefully, making a full stop before she entered the stream of holiday traffic.

I was tired from just *looking* at her. I climbed into my car and rested for a few minutes before I resumed my errands. It was easy to predict the rest of her day: she'd go home, unload the car and the kids, change some diapers, fix lunch, put the kids down for a nap, wrap some gifts while they slept, address some cards, fix a snack when the children woke up, take them — and the dog —for a walk, settle the little ones with some toys in front of the TV, keep an eye on the five-year-old in the backyard and prepare dinner . . .

After dinner she'd clean up the kitchen, bathe the children, tell them bedtime stories and hear their prayers, and then she'd "relax" in front of the TV while she folded a mountain of laundry.

I started to hyperventilate with a case of extreme empathy. Not too many years ago I had been doing the same things. With three babies in four years, I had coped with limited money, limited time, "chicken pops," "cradle cap" and sibling battles that made World War II look like a sock hop.

In an era when corporations moved employees around like checkers on a board, I had moved five times in seven years, each time earnestly seeking out other women with small children, asking the names of their pediatricians, their dentists, their psychiatrists.

The station wagon was my second home, constantly in and out of the driveway with trips to the grocery store, church and doctor. Who could forget those days: A little girl who fell backward onto a needle that narrowly missed her lung; a five-year-old who tasted some crusty acid that had been scraped off a car battery in the driveway; two kids with asthmatic bronchitis in oxygen tents at the same time.

And later, three children whose tonsils "must come out," or so I was told. One of them swallowed the Aspergum she'd been given after the sugery and we had to race back to the doctor to be certain it wasn't lodged in her throat . . . The child whose knee painfully locked in an hysterical reaction but who was afraid to tell us, once the ambulance had arrived, that the knee had *unlocked.*

And through it all I continued to put decent meals on the table, and keep the kids and house reasonably clean. Admittedly, I never approached award-winning standards but I managed to give parties, sometimes taught Sunday school and always wrote my mother.

As for Christmas, the stockings got hung, the gifts wrapped, the cookies baked (or purchased) and only once did I find my carefully addressed Christmas cards neatly tucked away — unmailed — in January.

So how come, now that I have no babies crawling around the kitchen floor, no tiny tots tugging at my hem, and no school children asking for help with their arithmetic — how come I am totally exhausted by a chance encounter with a young mother in a check-out line?

Note Space for Mom

55
Even-Steven

I was in a small bakery, pouring myself a coffee-to-go, when I heard the woman next to me order hot cross buns and "two MATCHING chocolate donuts."

"Kids?" I asked, as I poured cream into my cup.

"Yeah," she said with a guilty laugh, "even at 15."

"Ha," said I, "even at 30."

Darn! Once again I'd revealed to a total stranger that I was older than 39, but it didn't matter. As mothers of children only 15 years apart, we understood each other perfectly. We understood that it's a lot easier to buy perfectly matched donuts than it is to evenly divide our attention, caring and love.

When my kids were younger, I remember envying the parents of an only child. It wasn't that their house was cleaner or quieter, that there was no bickering or fighting over toys. No, their biggest advantage was that whenever they did something for that child, they were not SETTING PRECEDENT.

I, on the other hand, was faced with dire consequences every time I made a decision. If Patty at age 7 was mature enough for a two-wheeler, it meant that I'd better be ready to hand over a two-wheeler to Peggy when she hit the same age. If Peggy begged for and got gymnastics lessons at age 8, then I'd better be ready to deal with karate lessons for David when he hit that magic number.

It became apparent very early on that every time I granted a favor or request it was going to come back to haunt me, while parents of only one child were allowed the luxury of making decisions based on intuition and impulse. They were even allowed to FORGET what they'd decided earlier. With the shrewd negotiators I was raising, it soon became clear that I'd have to keep a mental set of books to make sure no one was over-indulged or short-changed.

However, my goal of even-handed child-rearing ran head-on into the vastly different personalities of three vastly different kids. Sure, I could always divide half of a cherry pie into three perfectly matched pieces, but the rest of life was more complicated than that.

Both girls were crazy about horses, but their budget (with a little parental help) barely allowed for the upkeep of one. Sharing a well-loved animal sometimes led to harsh words and well-placed shoves, but Mom was usually on hand to arbitrate.

David spent his formative years watching his older sisters and learning. He developed sure-fire methods for getting just about anything he needed or wanted. During those growing-up years I had to figure out who really needed help with homework and who was taking advantage. I learned when to loan money and when to declare it a gift.

These days I still offer advice and counsel when asked, and try to keep my mouth shut otherwise. When life is easy for one of my kids but hard for another, I pray for things to even out a little. But sometimes I wish I could just give them three magic matching donuts. Only then would life be fair — "Even-Steven," as the kids used to say.

56
Slow Children at Play

I was out nagging the flowers the other morning, lopping off a branch here, pinching back a shrub there, and as usual, wearing slippers. You see, if I even put my nose out the door on a fresh summer morning, it's very difficult to get me back into the house to the chores of laundry, dishes and vacuuming.

That explains why I do most of my gardening in a nightgown and robe, and why my neighbors frequently come close to calling the law, thinking I am an escapee from a funny farm.

But as I was saying, I was snipping off a few roses when a memory from childhood overcame me. I looked around to make sure that no one was watching, then with thumb and forefinger, I broke off a very large rose thorn, licked the bottom of it and stuck it on my nose!

That's right, on my nose!

When I was a kid, we used to put thorns on our noses and pretend we were dragons or some kind of prehistoric monster, and I just wanted to see if I could still do it.

Naturally, I removed it before I came back into the house (*they* think I'm an old dragon anyhow) but it started me thinking about the things we do as children that we can no longer do as adults without risking great embarrassment.

Summer, it seemed to me, was the logical time for such

childish experiments. Free from the schedule of school bells and unfettered by clothes that must be kept clean, we wandered and explored the wonders of our own back yards, but that was a time when back yards were not manicured gems of landscaping. There were plenty of patches of just plain dirt, tall weeds in which to hide, and very few fences separating one neighbor from another.

Out in the dirt we built whole cities with twisting roads and tunnels for our toy cars, refuges for ladybugs and ants, and "hideouts" for our treasures. We practiced the ancient art of whistling on a blade of grass or making music with a tissue and a comb, and after supper there were falling stars to count and ghost stories to be told.

It seems as if today's kids have lost those freedoms. Parents get concerned if their offspring are not accounted for every minute. "What on earth are they *doing*" is the reaction these days if a bunch of kids disappear behind a tree. In my mother's era, the disappearance of the children for a half hour was cause for celebration.

Today's youngsters have a very different kind of summer. With many of their parents working full time, they are shuttled off to computer classes, tennis camp, ballet lessons and diet spas. Only the underprivileged are unsupervised, and often they must stay indoors for their own protection.

Some kids have never left their spot in front of the TV set long enough to go outdoors and watch the sun set. Most have never squeezed nectar from a honeysuckle blossom and savored its sweetness. And I guess it goes without saying that few have put rose thorns on their noses, pretending to be fire-breathing dragons.

57
Coming Clean

You know you haven't raised bad kids when they come to visit and say, "Mom, if there's anything I can help you with, let me know."

It's a nice change from when they were teens and I had to lie in wait and snag them before they got out to the car. And so when Son recently came to visit, I sat sipping my coffee, waiting for him to wake up and help me prune the oak tree. I was just pouring my second cup when I heard the splash of the shower. The scent of shampoo wafted out to the kitchen long before the young man himself appeared.

What a picture he was! Fresh shirt, fresh jeans, fresh hair. No one in his right mind would suggest that this shiny creature climb up into the old worm-ridden oak tree and generate a cloud of sawdust. The pruning job was out of the question.

When, I thought, can a parent ask any physical, sweaty and unpleasant work from a child when the reply is bound to be, "But Mom, I'm all clean!" And *when* did the morning shower replace the evening bath for most American families? It must have been just about the same time that anti-perspirants, deodorant soap and hair conditioners were invented. "Cleanliness is next to Godliness" was not a new idea, but cleanliness as a religion was, and the high priest was television.

To my way of thinking, they've got it all backward. When I

grew up, we spent the day getting un-clean. If we had yard chores, we put on our old clothes, and while we certainly washed our hands and faces for dinner, bath time came after homework and before bed. Then we took our still-warm bodies and climbed between sheets that had dried on the clothesline and smelled like sunshine. True, we may have used our bath towels for several nights in a row, but they were usually clean because they'd dried clean bodies.

Today's younger generation goes directly from bed to shower in the morning, employing a myriad of cleansing agents and appliances along the way to assure that they are socially acceptable whether they work behind a desk or under a car. If their day's work requires some physical exertion, they will almost certainly bathe again before going out in the evening, and I'll lay odds that they grab a fresh towel no matter how many times they shower.

Paradoxically, at the end of the day most young adults will then fall into a bed that was left unmade and into which they have laid an unwashed body for the past X-number of nights. Since they sleep as if they were dead, it doesn't seem to matter.

On Monday mornings after I've had the younger generation for the weekend, I amuse myself by imagining what would happen if, through time travel, we transported these same offspring to the era when baths were a luxury and a "Saturday Night Special" was more likely to be the whole family sharing a tub, one at a time.

Father, the breadwinner, bathed first, followed by Mother. Then the children, from oldest to youngest, stepped gingerly into the same water which, if they were lucky, might be warmed a bit from a kettle on the woodstove.

One or two towels served for all, and soap — far from being "Ivory gentle" — had a bit of sting it. The only way to stay warm was to sleep three to a bed, and on a frosty night the kids made a shivering dash from the tepid tub to the quilt-covered four-poster.

On the following Sunday morning, they pulled on their clothes as fast as they could, splashed some icy water onto their faces, and appeared for a breakfast of hot oatmeal.

No languid shower, no steaming bathroom mirror, no deodorant mist or hair spray in the air, no once-used towels left on the floor.

Why, I wonder, do we now think of ourselves as being so very dirty that we must spend millions of dollars and trillions of gallons of water to make ourselves clean?

Note Space for Mom

58
Kids! Need Cash?

Get a load of the ad I found in the paper today! Do you think it means something's going on that we ought to know about?

CASH!
Kids! Need cash for the holidays?
Your clothing (to size 10) & toys
By appointment

(A store name and phone number followed.)

Call me alarmist but I definitely see a problem here. I envision thousands of kids, ages 1 to 10, methodically rifling through their closets, drawers and toy boxes, filling up plastic garbage bags, and hopping a bus to this enterprising merchant. There they'll unload all that unnecessary kid-stuff Mom and Dad have been saving — the baby shoes, silver spoons, stuffed bears, Lincoln logs, music boxes and Lego toys — sentimental junk no self-respecting Nintendo player has any use for.

Over the counter will go the Winnie-the-Pooh raincoats, the Mickey Mouse hats, the Roger Rabbit T-shirts. It's all outgrown anyway, and so what if Mom's still in the child-bearing years; any new sibling isn't going to want a bunch of old hand-me-downs. Every kid knows that. And if it's worth a few bucks, why not?

This might not be such a bad idea on the surface. After all, most of us are packrats by nature and some of us even hire people to help us muck out our lives now and then. But children, as we know, have a tendency to over-do things. Once the kids have cleaned out their own space and realized a little income for their efforts, they may start looking around for new possibilities. . .

Doesn't Mom have an old fur coat she's hiding somewhere because she's too environmentally conscious to wear it out on the street? And what about those flowered shirts of Dad's, the ones left over from the '60s that he's saving for the '90s. Of course, all this stuff is going to be larger than a child's size 10 but an enterprising kid could find at least two or three outlets in town.

Parents, busy as they are, may not notice that they suddenly have extra closet space. They'll just chalk it up to being adult and orderly. However, at this point we have a youngster who, just as he's beginning to understand how the free enterprise system works, is running out of clothes to sell. Hmmmmm. Looking around, he sees that there are far too many pictures on the walls of his house, a number of small artifacts the folks have accumulated from their travels, and some old costume jewelry Mom never wears.

He also notes that Dad has at least three sets of golf clubs and probably wouldn't miss one of them. Moving out to the garage, he finds a treasure trove of stuff — weights, an exercise bike, a set of ratchet wrenches and a cobweb-covered power saw.

Once again our young entrepreneur will have to consult the Yellow Pages to find buyers, but no problem; he was checking there anyway to find out how to rent a truck.

Yes, as I said earlier, we may have a serious problem. Inviting kids to sell their clothing and toys for cash may be only the tip of the iceberg. Parents should perhaps take steps to see that the trend goes no further. Hubcaps that lock and car alarms that shriek may not be enough; keeping your automobile pink slip in a vault may not be enough. It might not even be a bad idea to keep the deed of trust on your home with a friend. That is, unless your friend also has a wily growth-oriented executive in the nursery, or a 5-year-old who's looking for venture capital.

As for you O. Henry-type optimists out there, the ones who adore the idea of a child selling his most precious possessions in order to buy a Christmas gift for his mother or father . . . I have a bridge you might be interested in buying.

What bridge, you ask?

The one that Dad left soaking in a glass of Polident last night.

WAITING
ROOM

59
The Waiting Game

Local police departments are warning residents to be on the lookout for strangers, especially anyone who sits waiting in a parked car for no apparent reason. The theory is that it might be a burglar's "look-out" or even a molester lying in wait for some unsuspecting victim.

More than likely it's just another mother waiting for a child who's having ballet lessons, playing soccer or having his orthodontic appliance adjusted.

I speak from experience. If I had a dime for every hour I've spent waiting for kids, I'd be a rich — and tired — woman. As it is, I'm just tired.

I've waited at elementary school front doors while the children escaped out the back gate. I've sat in downpours outside intermediate schools waiting for kids who caught a ride with another mother.

I've sat in the waning twilight of a winter day waiting for a high school athlete to run just one more lap, and done time at the doctor's, the dentist's, the counselor's; at charm schools, orthopedists and x-ray labs. I recognize every issue of National Geographic that was printed after 1959.

I've roamed the library while a child researched dinosaurs, sat outside roller-skating rinks till closing, and even huddled in my car in the dark, parked up the street and out of sight, while my too-young-to-drive son delivered a good-night kiss to his sweetheart.

I've waited outside county buildings while civil service exams were given, and outside companies where job interviews were in progress. I've lingered in department stores, waiting for a young shopper, until the security guards became suspicious.

I've hung around road-racing tracks, Toys-R-Us's and electronic-game parlors; lurked outside miniature golf courses and "cruised the Main" till movies ended.

I've waited for anesthetic to wear off, shoes to be fitted, ears to be pierced, dimes to be spent. I've waited for eyes to dilate, guitars to be re-strung, interest to be added, and mantras to be bestowed. I've waited outside hospital rooms, oxygen tents, Star Trek stores, and Sunday School doors.

Men often ask what women do with all their spare time since the invention of so many labor-saving devices. The answer is obvious:

They loiter.

60
Busy, Busy, Busy

I stood at the teller's window, papers in hand, prepared to borrow from Peter to pay Paul. A woman moved into line at the next window. I glanced up, glanced away again, intent on the business at hand.

A moment later the woman stepped over to me and said very tentatively, "Bev?"

"Yes. Hi. Hello," I stammered as I tried to put a name with the face. How embarrassing. It was my neighbor, one who lives almost directly across the street from me. "How *are* you?" I asked, and we both laughed at the absurdity of people living so near each other but at such a distance. We made small talk, then both went back to our errands and exchanged a wave of farewell.

It wasn't so long ago that she moved into my neighborhood, perhaps eight or nine years. I had introduced myself and we even had a few outings together. My son had been her sitter back then.

As I drove away from the bank, I thought about how nice it would be to have lunch with her again and catch up on the events in her life. The very next thought was of all the others I should get together with: Tina, Betty, Sheila, Sandra, Joan and a dozen others.

So why don't I call them? And why don't they call me?

I think we're all just too busy. I don't know anyone who

isn't working outside the home or attending school, and when we see each other, we usually say, "Let's have lunch."

It's not an empty phrase. I think we all would sincerely love to take an hour or two out of our schedules to relax with an old friend but somehow it doesn't happen. We're all out in the world, rubbing elbows like mad, but at the same time we're cut off. Gone are the days when we had time for the lengthy kaffee klatsch and the hair-letting-down sessions.

In those days the kids played at our feet and interrupted so incessantly that conversation had to be wedged in between trips to the potty, wiping noses or settling disputes over the ownership of toys.

We couldn't wait to get the little critters off to school and out of our hair. We wanted free time for tennis, shopping and lunching with friends.

Kindergarten provided little relief. It seemed that the kids went off to school each morning and there was only time for scanning the newspaper and enjoying an uninterrupted shower before they were back at the door, eager to show their drawings. As each child came along, the schedule got crazier. "Early Birds," "Late Birds," field trips, rainy day schedules.

As the kids got bigger, we got busier. Scouts, Parent's Club, chauffeuring kids to soccer, swim meets and ballet lessons. Later, a lot of us joined the work force, and the juggling of responsibilities became even more complicated.

Now the habit of constant activity is strong. It almost seems decadent to actually plan a lunch hour of leisure. Shouldn't we be running erands or picking up the cleaning?

The answer, my friends, is NO. Life is short. Pick up the phone, call an old friend and invite her to lunch. I'll do the same.

Note Space for Mom

MOTHERING HEIGHTS (AND DEPTHS) is available through local bookstores that use R. R. Bowker Company BOOKS IN PRINT catalog system. Order through publisher SUNFLOWER INK for bookstore discount.

TO ORDER INDIVIDUAL COPIES, please fill out coupon below:

Make check payable to:
Beverly Borgman
P.O. Box 4402
Carmel, CA 93921

______	BOOKS AT $8.00 PER COPY	$	________
	6½% SALES TAX (CA RES.)		________
	SHIPPING AND HANDLING		2.00
	TOTAL	$	________

NAME ______________________________

ADDRESS ______________________________

CITY ______________ STATE ______ ZIP ________
